CW00683613

no
worries
if n😊t

no worries if not

A FUNNY (ISH) STORY OF GROWING UP WORKING CLASS AND QUEER

Soph Galustian

RADAR

First published in Great Britain in 2023 by Radar, an imprint of
Octopus Publishing Group Ltd
Carmelite House
50 Victoria Embankment
London EC4Y 0DZ
www.octopusbooks.co.uk

An Hachette UK Company
www.hachette.co.uk

Distributed in the US by
Hachette Book Group
1290 Avenue of the Americas
4th and 5th Floors
New York, NY 10104

Distributed in Canada by
Canadian Manda Group
664 Annette St.
Toronto, Ontario, Canada M6S 2C8

ISBN 978-1-80419-008-1

A CIP catalogue record for this book is available from the British Library.

Printed and bound in the United Kingdom

10 9 8 7 6 5 4 3 2 1

Typeset in 9/13.5pt Farnham Text by Jouve (UK), Milton Keynes

This FSC® label means that materials used for
the product have been responsibly sourced.

Illustrations by Jayde Perkin

I dedicate this book to my nephew, Luke x

In this book I've referenced the music that has been the
soundtrack to my best, worst and most memorable times.
Some songs on this playlist are iconic and others not so much.
Back then, I was either dry humping or crying my eyes out
to some of the bangers the 00s/10s had to offer...
I hope you enjoy them as much as I did.

No worries if not x

Introduction

I'm Soph, not Sophie. When I order a coffee from Starbucks and I tell them my name is Soph, they reply with 'Is that Sophie?' When I sign off an email 'Best Wishes, Soph' and the reply is 'Thanks for your email, Sophie' – I don't recall saying Sophie, so STOP. It's Soph. Just Soph. Obviously, if you want to get into the nitty gritty of it, my passport says Sophie, and my mum calls me Sophie when I'm in trouble, but unless you're my passport or my mum, Soph will do! I find it's more approachable and friendly and makes me feel good. I'm halfway to fifty, very gay and slightly depressed. My hobbies include being sexy, talented and funny. I enjoy nights in and nights out. During job interviews in which we all had to share an 'interesting fact' about ourselves, I used to enjoy creating the most memorable lie in the room. My last lie was that I got through to the live shows of *The X Factor*, but couldn't go because I was on holiday. Both of those things are untrue – and for all you know, I could even be lying now! That's the beauty of it, but you've already bought my book now, so thank you – unless you're standing in the middle of Tesco, reading the first page and weighing up whether or not to get it. (Go on. Don't be snide.)

People often ask my girlfriend, 'How do you put up with her?', and people often say to my family, 'I bet she was 'ard work growing up.' I couldn't tell you what led them to believe I was that much of a handful, but I suppose we can unravel my larger-than-life characteristics here, on the page.

1

Before we get proper into this, though, I feel like you should know that I'm a Manc (someone from Manchester) through and through. If you are too, you won't have an issue understanding any of this book. However, if you don't have the *luxury* of being northern, here's a little dictionary explanation of our slang. Please feel free to refer to it when you have no idea what I'm talking about:

Angin' – Absolutely horrible. Example: 'Boris Johnson is *angin'*.'

Mither – To bother or annoy someone. Example: 'Stop *mithering* me.'

Peck 'ed – Someone who's doing my head in. Example: 'You're such a *peck 'ed*, you.'

Dead – Extremely. Example: 'I'm *dead* hungry, me.'

Mint – Very good. Example: 'Wow, Jodie Comer is *mint*.'

Snide – Ungenerous. Example: 'The Tories are *snide*.'

Mingin' – Revolting. Example: 'The pasta from the canteen was absolutely *mingin'*.'

Buzzin' – Extremely happy. Example: 'I'm *buzzin'* to be writing a book.'

Get on this – You'll never guess what. Example: '*Get on this*, I've been sacked.'

Swear down – I am absolutely telling the truth, the whole truth and nothing but the truth. Example: 'My dog ate my homework, I *swear down*.'

Our kid – Literally anybody that you know and like. Example: 'Alright *our kid*. Long time, no see.'

Ee are – Excuse me. Example: '*Ee are*, move.'

Scav – Someone who tries to take you for everything they can get. Example: 'Gis a quid' or 'Can I try some of those crisps?'

Give your 'ed a wobble – You need to have a rethink. Example: 'You voted Brexit? *Give your 'ed a wobble*, pal.'

Gaff – House. Example: 'The bailiffs are round our *gaff*.'

Knock on – Knocking on your mate's gaff to see if they're playing out. Example: 'I'm *knockin' on* for Gem.'

Clock on – Somebody noticing something. Example: 'Everyone's *clocked on* that I'm a lezza.'

'ave it – A celebration. Example: 'You won a BAFTA? Let's *'ave it*.'
Bobbins – Rubbish. Example: 'Our government chat *bobbins*.'
Me – Always added to the end of a sentence. Example: 'I love *Corrie*, *me*.'

Don't you think the beginning of something is always the most fuckin' annoying part? I dread starting literally *anything*. A series, **a book**, exercise . . . *starting* something new is only mildly better than *trying* something new – like when you decide to get something different from the Chinese that you haven't tried before, and it ends up being shite, and you wish you'd stuck to the salt-and-pepper chips, like the predictable and safe girly you are. I read somewhere once that it's because of anxiety, but I think I don't like it for two reasons. The first reason is that I'm sometimes scared of taking a risk and it not paying off – if I started a new series and it ended up being a load of bobbins, I'd be devastated. That's why I've watched *Stranger Things* series one to four a grand total of six times. There's thirty-four episodes all together, and they're roughly around an hour long. Now, I failed my Maths GCSE (three times); however, Google tells me that's a total of 204 hours, or eight and a half days of watching twelve-year-olds chase Demogorgons. I'm happy with that; I'm comfortable with it. I know what's going to happen, and I like it. The second reason would be because I'm a lazy cow. Maybe we can work it out together as we stumble through this book I'm currently writing? I mean, I hope it'll be finished by the time you're reading it, but hey – stranger things have happened.

Pun intended.

I can't lie, it feels like an out-of-body experience, knowing that I am writing a book. When I was a kid, I didn't really read a lot (just being honest), and when I did read, it was just the Argos catalogues around Christmas. I read the prices; anything more than £20 wasn't granted a circle. Santa couldn't afford it. After all, he was buying every child on the planet something from either Argos or Toys R Us, so . . . I think I also read the first five pages of a *Goosebumps* book once – don't ask me which one. It was the first and last book I borrowed from the library.

I think I'd recently watched *Matilda*, and wanted to copy that wholesome scene where she goes to the library with a little trolley and fills it with books and reads them all. My library experience didn't quite live up to the film. I took one of the *Goosebumps* books home and it gathered dust under my bed, and then my dog at the time, Annie, pissed all over it. Maybe she knew I just wasn't that into it? She was such a good girl with a bad bladder problem. May she rest in peace. So basically, I never returned the book. OK – there, I said it! I'm a thief. I couldn't possibly return the piss-soaked book to the little old librarian lady who I never heard talk.

If someone asked what job I'd be crap at, it would be working in a library. It would be a lot of jobs, to be honest, but especially working in a library. It's just too peaceful in there. I'd purposefully cause chaos due to boredom. Maybe if I'd returned the book, I might have heard the librarian talk? Maybe she would have shocked me and said something like, 'You silly little bitch, you can't bring a book back soaked in dog piss!' imagine that. I never paid my fine. I think it was something like £6, which, to a nine-year-old in 2006, is like a grand. That would have bought me sixty Freddos before inflation took over (thanks for the maths, Google). So, Cheadle Library staff, if you're reading this – I'm sorry. I'll pop in next time I'm about and pay my fine. Promise. As long as I haven't built up any arrears. It's here in writing for you.

I tried reading *Harry Potter* and *Hunger Games*, but I quickly gave up and just popped the films on instead. Easier, innit? If you're one of those snobs who say, 'Oh, the book is better' – respectfully, fuck you. I don't have a very good attention span. I've stopped and started this paragraph alone *four* times. Three of those times, I've investigated the fridge. Surprisingly, nothing new has appeared in there. I tell you what we've got a lot of, though: rosé. Rosé for days. How nutritious.

So, I was never destined to become a librarian. My teachers at school used to say, 'She's a bright girl. She just needs to know when to keep her gob shut.' Which I think is rude, as I provided nothing but laughs. Even the teachers would laugh, which, of course, only encouraged me more.

One of my teachers told my mum at parents' evening that I'd 'amount to nothing'. My mum kicked the fuck off. I sat there, smug, thinking, *Go on girl, you tell him*. I can appreciate now I was a little shit in his class and caused him a lot of issues, as well as distracting everyone else, but telling a fourteen-year-old she'll amount to nothing is, well, harsh. His class was boring, to be fair, and he had the most monotonous voice. You could never tell his emotions; all of them looked the same. A bit like Kristen Stewart in *Twilight*: *lifeless*. But yes, I would still shag her. His classroom was right outside the canteen as well, so the second I smelled that plastic-looking, greasy pizza – I was on one. I wish he'd known then that I'd go on to write a bloody book. I wish I'd known that I'd go on to never use Pythagoras again. Fuck Pythagoras.

A book! I know I haven't stopped going on about it, but little me wouldn't believe this is happening. Here's a conversation between Big Soph and Little Soph, for some context:

BIG SOPH

Hey, Little Soph, what do you think about people that write books?

LITTLE SOPH

Clever, boring and rich.

BIG SOPH

I can see why you'd say that. How would you feel if I told you that we go on to write a book of our own one day?

LITTLE SOPH

Oh, don't talk rubbish, Big Soph. There's no chance.

BIG SOPH

Honestly. It's just a misconception that you have to be rich, clever and/or boring to write a book. When I say a misconception, I mean it's *our* wrong opinion. It's OK, though, because we'll grow out of it.

As a working-class northerner, we've been programmed to believe that the prospect of writing a book will always be unachievable. We think we're destined to be a housewife who prepares Spam for her husband after a long day earning minimum wage.

LITTLE SOPH

Have you swallowed a dictionary or something? Also, we don't even like Spam.

BIG SOPH

It's true. Statistically, we are unlikely to go on and become an author. But hey, fuck the statistics! We're doing it, baby. We'll also be pretty alright at writing poetry. I know we don't like Spam, but we thought our husband probably would.

LITTLE SOPH

Poetry? Do you mean like Shakespeare and that? Don't know if I want a husband, Big Soph.

BIG SOPH

Not really. We write kind of modern poetry. Some poems are funny, others are moving. They'll basically piece together bits of our life so far. Like the time we accidentally killed our goldfish. Oh, and don't worry about the husband thing . . . we're gay!

LITTLE SOPH

I'd really prefer if you didn't bring up the goldfish . . . Wait, we're WHAT?!

BIG SOPH

Sorry. And I know! We're into girls. But you already knew that, didn't you, Little Soph?

LITTLE SOPH

I mean, yes I did know. We do snog posters of Girls Aloud on our wall, after all. So, you're telling me that we end up becoming some sort of writer?

BIG SOPH

I'd really prefer if you didn't bring up the Girls Aloud posters . . . And yes, that's exactly what I'm telling you. We are a writer! We write mostly comedy (very us), but other stuff, too.

LITTLE SOPH

What does Mum reckon of that?

BIG SOPH

She's buzzin'. Very proud of us. Everyone is!

LITTLE SOPH

What does Dad reckon of us being gay?

BIG SOPH

He's sweet with it. Doesn't mind, just wants us to be happy.

LITTLE SOPH

Cool. Do we have a mansion with a swimming pool?

BIG SOPH

Not yet, but we might get there one day. We do have a TV in our bedroom, though – with Freeview. We've always wanted that.

LITTLE SOPH

True. Are we happy?

BIG SOPH

. . . We're getting there, kid. We're getting there.

Bless Little Soph. There's a lot she's going to go through. Experiences that will shape her, make her, and ones that will most definitely break her – but I guess that's life. You might have gathered from all this that I write poetry. I didn't really know I could do it until I did it; I think that's the case with most things. I was on the 381 bus to Waterloo during the peak of my depression, listening to Lukas Graham through my earphones and just writing my feelings down in the notes app on my phone. I didn't mean for it to rhyme at first, but once I'd started, it kind of just came naturally. A bit like when you go for a wee and then a poo comes out that you didn't plan. Is that a wanky thing to say? Not the poo comment – that's down to earth, and true. I mean the fact that poetry came naturally to me. I didn't know I had this skill until I started writing. It was like unzipping all my emotions that had been bursting at the seams for so long. It was such a release. Stronger than any therapy I've ever had. I think I got off the bus to go to work, and then changed my mind and got straight back on it going the other way. I didn't want the flow to end. I find that I write better when I don't plan stuff. Again, that could be a sign of laziness . . . or just my creative process (definitely wanky). But before I knew it, I had a full spoken-word poem in front of me: one that I, somehow, had written.

It stayed in my notes app for a few months before I opened it again. It was in between a note titled '*X Factor* favourite auditions' and 'Dad's NHS number'.

I know you'll automatically be wondering what my favourite *X Factor* auditions are (but not my dad's NHS number). There are twenty-two on my list. I might tell you some more in a bit, but here's my top three:

Rachel Lester – Unemployed icon from Cardiff. Been all around the towns and everything.

Ariel Burdett – Wanted a scrap with Cheryl. Holistic vocal coach. Recently passed away. RIP.

Holly Jervis – Big, blonde and beautiful. Simon called her 'cave mouth'. From the sunny Isle of Wight.

One of my talents is reciting *X Factor* auditions word for word. I can't escape living in my 2010 *X Factor* era. It was so iconic, for so many reasons. I miss that time. I tell you what I don't miss from 2010, though . . . my hair. It was so shit.

Anyway, back to my sad poem. I feared opening that note and rereading it. I didn't want to make myself vulnerable if I was having an OK mental health day. I wanted to save it for a day when I felt like shit, so I could do what everyone enjoys doing – making themselves feel *worse* 😵. That day eventually came, and I forced myself to open the note. I read it maybe five or six times. I decided I might want to share it with someone, but I felt as though just words written down didn't hold enough weight. I wanted someone to hear me say it. I felt like it would have more meaning that way. So, I waited for some good natural lighting, and stuck my phone to the window with Sellotape. So, I filmed it. It took me six takes; I cried for three of them. I didn't want to show anyone footage of me crying. (There was once a video that I uploaded on a website back in the day called Keek, of me screaming-crying when Cheryl (Cole) followed me on Twitter in 2012. That's a whole other can of beans that I'll probably get on to at some point. Anyway, I never lived it down. It's the ugliest crying video on the planet. I'm bright red, covered in snot and tears. It was pre-braces, so my teeth are *angin'*. It's a haunting image. Don't even *try* and find it on Google, it's GONE! I made bloody well sure of that before writing this, let me tell you.)

On the sixth take, I nailed it. No crying, no fuck-ups, no sound of my next-door neighbour singing 'Sweet Caroline' for the thirteenth time that day. Just me and my words.

I should probably tell you that '381' is about my experience of grief. It's very honest about how shit and difficult grief is. How it's consuming, how it takes over everything you thought you knew about life and love. It's a feeling you can't describe. The deepest, darkest depths of pain. Not only is it mentally painful, but the physical pain that it brings can make you feel like you're dying. Literally. I remember thinking I was having a heart attack because my chest was in so much pain. I didn't know that heartbreak can physically *hurt* your heart. Don't you think that's crazy? We can love someone so much that when they're taken away from us, we physically ache for them.

I think loss is the only thing in the world we cannot control. Most of our day-to-day issues have solutions, or we eventually get over them. Didn't get the job you went for? Oh well, try again next time. Husband cheated on you? Time is a healer. Broke your leg? It'll heal. Shit happens. You get my gist. There is no solution for loss, though. No quick fix. You cannot bring that person back. You cannot rewind time. There is *nothing* you can do for grief. I absolutely hate it when people say, 'It'll get easier.' How *dare* you tell me that the loss of my fourteen-year-old nephew will 'get easier'? How *dare* you tell me that you 'lost your ninety-four-year-old nan last year' so you 'know how it feels'? Rule number one when discussing grief: *never* try and compare your grief with someone else's. It's fucking annoying, insensitive and self-absorbed.

So, there I was, deciding who to send my sad-as-fuck poem to. I weighed up the options.

> **Mum** – She'll defo put it on Facebook within three minutes of receiving it. No.
> **Dad** – Doesn't know I'm on antidepressants. Might have a heart attack. No.
> **Brother** – Emotionally unavailable. No.
> **Girlfriend at the time** – Will love it. Loves anything I do. Too complimentary. No.
> **Friends** – Will ask me if I'm OK. No.
> **Sister** – I don't know how she'll react. Her opinion means the most to me. Yes.

I asked her if she wanted to see it first. A bit like a trigger warning, I gave her the gist of it. Told her it's a bit emoshy. (A fun way I like to deal with my trauma is to shorten words to make them sound 'cute'. Other examples of this are 'depressedy' or, one of my personal favourites, 'suicidey'.)

Let me tell you something about my sister. She doesn't give compliments lightly – so when she does, you know she really means them. Unlike my mum; I could honestly look like a bag of warm shit and she'd be like, 'God, you're so stunning my girl xxxx.'

I'm not going to just keep calling her 'my sister' throughout this; her name is Stacey. (Mum loved it when people would sing that song 'Stacy's Mom'. Contrary to popular belief, it was released *after* our Stacey was born, but I have to say, Mum *has* got it going on.)

Anyway, here's how the conversation with Stacey went:

> Just listened to that god it was so sad bloody crying listening to it. Was so good though your words xxx

> Ah I'm so glad you like it <3 <3. That's all I wanted. Thanks for listening to it. Do you think I should share it? Or is too personal? Xxx

> It's up to you whatever you think xxx

> I don't know, kinda scared cause I cba with people that I don't like saying 'aw well done babe' and all that shit xxx

> I know what you mean xxx

11

I'll see anyway. I'm glad you like it that's all that mattered to me xxx

I really did listen to it twice and cried both times. The words are so so true what you say xxx

Yeah so true. Sometimes it's easier to say when I write it down. Decided that i'll share it, and any annoying comments sending love I'll just ignore ahah. Think that's OK? Xxx

Yes course just reply to who you want and fuck everyone else xxx

And so I did. I took the risk and I posted my poem online. I went to town: I put it on Instagram, Facebook and Twitter. The queens of social media. I was ready for my third cousins that I hadn't spoken to for the past ten years to comment something like 'Lots of love babes xx', and for people who barely knew me – and never knew my nephew, Luke – to say something like: 'He'd be so proud.' (That really fucks me off. Me and Stacey are always saying how annoying it is when people who aren't involved try and get involved. Especially family. You weren't arsed when it first happened, so don't pretend to be now. We're a good team like that; we get each other and we don't have time for anyone else's shit. My brother is the same. We're the three musketeers of taking no shit.)

Basically, what I'm trying to say is that I had no idea that two years (and 1.4 million views) later, I'd be here. On the page of this book, hopefully making you laugh, and maybe cry . . . Two of life's most gorgy emotions!

I feel like we should just start this off with '381', now that you've heard so much about it and its birth. Special shout-out to the 381 bus and my crippling depression – couldn't have done this one without you, girlies xxx.

381

'Life's too short': a phrase so often thrown around.
It had little meaning until I watched them put you into the ground.
One minute you're here and the next you're not.
Be grateful for every second that you've got.
'Time's a healer' just isn't true.
I didn't know that, until I lost you.

I'm going to try and use words to talk about grief.
About pain so painful, it's beyond belief.
About a knife stuck in your chest when you wake and when you rest.
A constant cloud heavy on your head.
You can't escape it, even when you go to bed.
You fall asleep 'cause you can't stand being awake.
You're exhausted from a reality that you face day to day.
The sad part is I see you in my dreams.
Everything is normal, I wake up and I could scream.
I close my eyes and I can't stand what I see.
An unfathomable image forever ingrained in me.
I look at my sister and I see nothing but pain,
but with a glimpse of you it's like I can't explain.
It's comforting, but at the same time it hurts;
seeing someone you love in pain, there's nothing worse.
I wish I could take her hurt away.
I remember holding your hand, begging you 'please stay'.
If I could sacrifice myself I would.
Fourteen years old, you barely left childhood.

I'm scared of the silence because I can hear the machines beeping.
It's masked by the sound of my loved ones weeping.
It's a sound that I just can't describe,
it's a haunting scream from deep inside.
The whole experience is like a record on replay,
I don't want to see it, but it just won't go away.
It makes me sick to my stomach when I reflect
the fact I'm here and you are not is entirely incorrect.
In the not-so silent silence, I sit and think of ways for
my mind to just stop.
There's one way out . . . but I'd have to sacrifice a lot.
I used to fear death, but that was before.
I can honestly say that I'm not scared any more.
This feeling had me praying to a god that I don't believe in,
to please just stop me from breathing.
I was down on my knees, I'm kneeling.
I didn't say bye, I didn't tell anyone I was leaving.

Sometimes I put my head in a pillow and I just start screaming.
I can't stand these feelings that I'm feeling.
People saying, 'Give it time, you'll start healing.'
If you believe that, you must be dreaming.
On the other hand, I'm thankful that my heart is still beating
'cause I keep you safe in here while time is fleeting.
I was going to end it all if it wasn't going to hurt our family.
But it will, so I'm trying to wait for it to come naturally.
I got so close to the edge before I regained my sanity.
My reality brought me back down to earth, I found my gravity.
When my time's up, we'll reunite in another galaxy.
Hopefully a place of happiness, no heartbreak or brutality.
No amount of time will ever heal me from this tragedy.
I hope for my loved ones and I hope for humanity
that we continue to be conscious of others' thoughts and feelings.

14

Some seem fine, and others are barely breathing, but you can't see it.
Be mindful of the people that are silent, the loud ones too.
Everyone is fighting their own battle,
including
me and you.

YOU KNOW THOSE BOOKS FULL OF BLANK PAGES,
WITH PROMPTS TO MANIFEST OR WRITE ABOUT YOUR
BIG DREAMS...? THIS ISN'T ONE OF THOSE BOOKS.
BUT LIKE ME ON THAT BUS, I DID WANT TO
PROVIDE SOME SPACE WHERE YOU CAN WRITE/
DRAW/CREATE, SO HERE IS A BLANK SPACE FOR YOU
TO REFLECT ON ANY THOUGHTS, FEELINGS OR
WORRIES THAT MAY HAVE ARISEN AFTER READING
THIS POEM. DRAW YOUR FEELINGS, WRITE A
SWEAR WORD, SKETCH A PAIR OF HAIRY BALLS.
DO WHATEVER YOU WANT — OR DON'T.

Childhood

It seems only right that we start at the beginning. Childhood! Woo hoo! Where all of our teeth fall out and all of our trauma is formed. How poetic. I'll tell you a bit about myself, if that's OK? No worries if not. x

OUR GAFF

I lived in a three-bedroom house in a little town called Cheadle, in Stockport. Our road was alright, you know. Half of it was made up of council houses; the other half was privately owned. Like some sort of weird class split down the middle. You could tell the council houses apart. They all had the same brown door. When I was a kid, I wondered if everyone's mum had borrowed the same can of paint to do their door. It seemed very boring to me – why did it all have to look the same? It's like saying, ''ey, look at us. We're on bennies.' All the private houses had massive doors with doorbells. Some of them had that posh stained glass leading into their porch. I bet they had umbrellas in there, a nice little shoe rack and coat pegs. Or maybe one of those doormats that say something like 'Welcome'. Welcome to what? Your porch? Thanks . . . (I don't know what I'd do if I had a porch. What are they *actually* for? They're always cold and stink of feet. 3/10 from me. I'm glad we didn't have one.)

You know what we had that they didn't, though? Double glazing.

I clearly remember the council coming to install double-glazed windows in our gaff. We were ahead of the posh houses! Every cloud.

I lived at home with just my mum for most of my life. Stacey moved out pretty young, and so did Matthew (my brother). We were alright until they introduced bedroom tax. Which, to my understanding, was the government charging households extra money if they had unoccupied bedrooms. After all, why shouldn't I, a socio-economically disadvantaged person, share my house with another socio-economically disadvantage person? In Maslow's eyes, I have absolutely no chance of reaching self-actualisation. Once bedroom tax came in, we had to get a lodger, which was fine, as Mum is a real people person. The more heads in the gaff, the better. She's a great hostess.

My mum and dad split up when I was two. They were married for eleven years. My mum still says to this day, she's never loved anyone else the way she loved my dad – which makes me feel all warm inside. I really can't imagine how they spent so long together, though. They're SO incredibly different – but hey, opposites attract, apparently. Also, this was in the days before social media, Tinder and sliding into people's DMs, so I think typically it was easier to spend a long time with someone. I always think it's so beautiful that I'm half my mum and half my dad. I like to study them both to figure out what personality traits of theirs I have. I have my dad's short temper and my mum's smile. My dad used to say to my mum, 'She'll have your beauty and my brains.'

Even though I was so little when they split up, I do have memories of my dad in the house – which means I've retained memories from being two years old. I didn't even know that was possible. I can remember the feel of his hair when I was a baby. He used to sit on the floor and watch football, and I'd sit behind him on the sofa, with my feet resting on his head. I thought I might have dreamed it, but my mum told me that's how we always used to sit. (I wish I could remember more from that age, like how blissful it must have been to not think of anything other than *Toy Story* and to sleep most of the day.)

Whatever I needed, my dad would always provide. I think him and my mum had some sort of deal that he wouldn't pay child maintenance, but would instead buy me anything I needed from the ages of two to eighteen, and I can safely say he *always* did. He wasn't rolling in it, BTW – far from it. He was a taxi driver, still is. So, he'd work his arse off all day to buy me the stuff that I needed when I was younger. I would have been a lot worse off without him.

I did see my dad, FYI. All the time, actually. He's amazing and I love him with my whole heart. Same goes for my mum. The best thing is, they're mates now. They spent a long time after they split up not talking to one another. I'd go between the two and listen to them slag each other off, which was always hurtful. It's not nice to hear someone you love being bad-mouthed by someone else you love, but I think their emotions were all over the place, and they probably both needed therapy – just like *most* people's parents do.

Ew, I can't believe I just said 'parents'. For me, the word 'parents' sounds posh and mingin'. I almost heave saying it. My mouth fills with saliva and I cringe, because I can't relate to having 'parents'. My posh friends all have 'parents'. When I picture 'parents', I imagine a mother, father, daughter and son, and a cute little spaniel doggy called Tilly, all sitting in a 'lounge' (again, fuckin' posh) with an open log fire, surrounded by chunks of wood they've collected from the garden. Having 'family time' on a Sunday evening, snacking on Pipers Karnataka Black Pepper & Sea Salt crisps, wearing buttoned-up cotton pyjamas from John Lewis, drinking Fortnum & Mason hot chocolates with Waitrose squirty cream in matching mugs, probably from Next homeware.

I imagine that their house is pristine, with Jo Malone diffusers in every room, and thick, soft carpet on the stairs – you know that carpet that feels like a mattress under your feet? They'd absolutely have that running through the gaff. They'd have a constant perfect room temperature throughout the house, and they'd ALWAYS have hot water. I bet the mum would open a bottle of red wine, have one glass and chuck the rest away because, well, she can. I bet the dad would have a brand-new car with heated seats, and he'd wear a Ralph Lauren gilet when it was cold outside. They'd own matching Tripp suitcases for all of their holidays to places like Thailand and America; they'd fly business class and drink champagne in one of those recliner seats. I bet they'd be able to afford to take Tilly (their spaniel dog, come on, keep up) away with them. I'd love to be able to take my pets on holiday with me. I think that's the only shite thing about a holiday, me, not being able to take your little stinky babies too.

OK fine, I got carried away. If you can relate to those things I've mentioned above, there is a chance you could be middle class. Not that there's anything wrong with that; I just don't fit into that world. That's why I hate the word 'parents', because all of the above couldn't be more alien to me. I think you could say part of me is jealous that some people have had that sheltered and cosseted life . . . I'm not in need of sympathy by the way, far from it. My childhood shaped the badass, working-class young lass that I am today (oh stop it, you, I know I can rhyme). We didn't have carpet in my gaff, but that was great, because if something was spilled, it would just dry and disappear (apparently), and we had a hand-me-down reclining leather sofa that was ideal because you could just wipe stuff off. The house smelled of cigs, dogs and wine, but do you know what? I wouldn't have had it any other way.

All of the plates and cups in my house were a mishmash; I think they were from my nanna back in the day, which was nice, because I love my nanna, so fuck your John Lewis matching sets. The times we didn't have electric to heat the house, we'd cuddle and get warm that way. I bet the rich people were too hot to cuddle, so every cloud, right? Growing up there allowed me to experience, appreciate and acknowledge situations and people from all walks of life, so technically, I'm thankful. I mean, some experiences I probably could have lived without . . . however, you wouldn't be reading this book if they hadn't happened, and I certainly wouldn't be writing it . . .

I think you deserve to know that my alien from the Argos catalogue never had babies. I tried so hard to mate her and she was having none of it. I don't know if she was infertile or just generally not maternal, but she really wasn't interested, and I'm a feminist, so I accepted her decision. It wasn't easy, but ultimately for the best.

TURKEY TWIZZLERS (PART ONE)

So, childhood. Where were we? One thing I miss a lot is Turkey Twizzlers. It was snide of Jamie Oliver to take those away from us and attempt to replace them with veg. That's a case for Childline, in my opinion. Yeah, they might have been bad or whatever, but my god – they tasted so *good*. I bet they were 25 per cent turkey, 75 poison, but I wasn't arsed, me; Turkey Twizzlers with beans and potato smileys was the ultimate tea. A tea for champions after a hard day at primary school making models out of playdough. Pissy Annie (library-book ruining dog) used to jump up and steal Turkey Twizzlers off my plate. It got so bad that sometimes I took my tea upstairs and ate with my pet fish, Bob; I didn't have to worry about him nabbing my food. (I did used to worry about him generally, though. Imagine living your whole life in a bowl in someone's bathroom. All you see is the same four walls, and people's constipated faces. What a life, eh?)

LYING (PART ONE)

When we're kids, we don't really think before we do or say almost anything – that's obviously because our brains aren't yet fully developed, and we're still learning how to process emotions and show empathy, etc. I think that's why a lot of kids lie. They're oblivious to what's realistic and what isn't. Apparently, the University of Waterloo carried out a study observing children in their own homes, and they found that 96 per cent of young children lie. Four-year-olds lie, on average, every two hours. Isn't that mad? What have you got to lie about when you're four?

Below are a few examples of lies that I told as a kid. Rated out of ten. Enjoy!

The *X Factor* lie

I once told my friends in primary school that for my birthday, I was going to be picked up in Simon Cowell's helicopter and flown to a special screening of *The X Factor* final before it had even happened. Then afterwards, we'd be going to Simon's house for fish and chips. I was only allowed to pick four friends, I explained to my group of six friends, so I'd only be picking who had been nicest to me that day.

Rating: The story was ruined by the part where I said we could watch *The X Factor* final before it had actually happened. It made the entire thing totally unbelievable. Disappointing. 5/10.

The voice-box lie

I convinced my next-door neighbours' kids that I could remove my voice box whenever I wanted to. I used to face away from them and make this funny noise, alluding to me putting my hand in my throat to simply take my voice box out. When it hit the outside air, it automatically became invisible, to protect itself. I would then mime to demonstrate how I could no longer talk, before swiftly reinserting it and finding my voice again.

Rating: I think this was really creative, and says a lot about my imagination. The story would have been a lot stronger if the voice box didn't become invisible when it was exposed to air. I want to know how that would have worked scientifically, as surely the voice box was exposed to air every time I opened my mouth? Some flaws in the narrative there. Good effort, nevertheless. 7/10.

The hearing-aid lie

I came into school with a singular earphone in my left ear. I had cut the wire off. When asked to remove it by my teacher, I said: 'It's a hearing aid. I can't take it out.' I was oblivious to the fact that my 'hearing aid' had 'SONY' written on the side of it. My teacher took it off me and then asked me, 'Do you think it's acceptable to pretend to be deaf?' I responded by shrugging, then wrote down on a piece of paper that I could no longer hear her because she'd removed my listening device. I got sent home.

Rating: This one took real confidence, and I admired my ability to keep up the lie despite being caught out. It shows great showmanship to my classmates. Very noble. 9/10.

BOYS CHASE THE GIRLS

So, we've established I was quite the fibber back in the day. I think it was mainly for attention, and to make my life sound cooler and more interesting than it was. People reckon that kids lie when they're going through something that they can't or don't want to vocalise. This was maybe the case with me, as I was trying to understand my sexuality at the tender age of around eight or nine. That might sound super early to some people, and maybe a little late to others. I find the whole idea of sexuality and discovering your sexuality so interesting. I think it's different for everyone. Some people discover their sexuality later in life; others are sure of themselves much earlier. I feel as though I was the latter. I have never felt anything different; my whole life has always been this way. Ever since I can remember, I've wanted to kiss girls, not boys.

Here are some questions I used to ask myself or wonder as a kid:

Are you born gay?

Do you become gay in the womb?

Do you become gay from being exposed to certain things in the media?

Can you control your desires to be gay?

Am I gay because my mum had a Caesarean? (Strange one, I know.)

Am I gay because my mum and dad got divorced?

Am I the only person in the world who feels this way?

Some of those questions sound wild, now I think about it. Why would being dragged out of my mum's stomach rather than her fanny make me gay? Interesting (sorry if you don't like the word fanny; I do, and it's my book). I would try and remember everything that had happened in my life up until that point, then attempt to figure out if any of it might have caused my sexuality. I think that's really sad. A lot of it was down to not having appropriate language to describe my feelings, nor the space to explore them at that young age. Some people might think that's for the best; they might say that, as children, we supposedly don't know what we want or like, because we're still developing, and so we're too young to make our own decisions. Part of me does understand that. However, not having that language and that space didn't change my sexuality or my narrative, it just suppressed it, and ultimately led to my internalised homophobia and shame, which took me a long time to unlearn. In fact, I am still unlearning some of it.

For me, back in the days of primary school, boys wore only blue and girls wore only pink. There were games such as 'boys chase the girls' or 'mummies and daddies', everyone was always focused on which boy fancied which girl, and we were taught the idea of straight marriage and straight sex. If you put any child in that restricted environment, they are always going to believe that anything that goes against those traditional values is different and wrong. Therefore, their feelings are wrong. *They* are wrong. Which is incredibly damaging later in life.

I'd never say my homelife played into me not being able to express my sexuality. It was just a case of what's 'normalised' in society. Nobody was gay in my family, and I very rarely heard of gay stories being told, nor did I see gay representation on TV. It was almost as if gay people didn't exist. That's why I find it funny when homophobes state that LGBTQ+ representation on TV is what causes children to 'think' they fit into that bracket. That is not how it works, *Karen*. One of my favourite films as a kid was *Labyrinth*. If you've seen this film, you'll know that everything about it is as far from reality as possible. Doorknobs speak to each other, and there's a worm who lives in a wall with his wife and gives people directions. After watching this film, I didn't then start asking worms in walls where big Tesco's was. Also, David Bowie's character was quite literally trying to date a child, but apparently there was no issue with exposing kids to that? Cool.

Parents (*gags*) need to stop blaming their children's sexuality or choices on what they're exposed to in the media. It does not work that way. If it did, I'd be very straight, as all I ever saw were heterosexual relationships, marriages and sex – and guess what? I *still* want nothing to do with a penis.

Also, kids have always used the word 'gay' as an insult. This didn't help in the world of acceptance. To be 'gay' was to be undesirable, weird, misunderstood. Nobody *chooses* to be those things. Growing up, you try your best to be anything but that. You're desperate to fit in. Equally, I believe it's impossible to change your sexuality. You like who you like, and it's as simple as that. If you believe that a person's sexuality is an issue, you're a massive knobhead.

When we played games like 'boys chase the girls', I used to make sure the numbers were uneven so I had to 'pretend to be one of the boys' and chase the girls. Is that funny? Or just sad? I think it's both. I also usually wore trousers to school; I was a stereotypical 'tomboy' at that time. So much so that one of my teachers told me I needed to stop hanging around with the boys, and make some friends in my year that were girls. This wouldn't be allowed now, but I remember it so clearly. I remember thinking, *Why can't I hang around with the boys? Why can't I wear trousers in the summer? Why can't I chase the girls?* All these questions were teaching me that my feelings were the issue. I'd put on this act at school to fit in with everyone else. My female friends and I would talk about the crushes we had on boys, while I would think about the crushes I had on girls. I never said anything, of course. I couldn't; there just wasn't the space for it.

KISSING (PART ONE)

I used to snog the back of my hand when I was a kid. I really hope I wasn't alone in this. I'd go home and close my eyes and imagine kissing a girl. While my lips were all over the back of my hand (which, ironically, had 'I <3 Connor' written on it – sorry Connor), I'd cup the hand I was kissing with my other hand and imagine I was holding the face of a girl, like I used to see in films.

I also used to believe you could get pregnant from mixing spit – hats off to any sex education I had at that age. Brilliant job. I thought I would end up being a young single mum after my first kiss. I'd even planned how I'd tell my mum. Luckily, my best friend Gemma, who was two years older (so obviously the oracle of all sexual knowledge), broke the news to me that it doesn't work that way. Thanks, Gem.

I had boyfriends in primary school. I was desperately trying to fit in. Of course, I never remotely liked these boyfriends. (Junaid, Aaron, Connor, Jordan, etc. – you're great . . . but you weren't for me). My first kiss was with a boy. (Apart from the kisses with my right hand and the disintegrating posters of female pop stars on my wall.) Unfortunately, it wasn't also my last kiss with a boy. Here's a poetic description of the gorgeous event. Shout-out to those who can relate:

Kissy

I watched him from across the playground
all of our mates gathered around.
He was having a pep talk off the boys,
they laughed and screamed, hyper, making noise.
His face was red
as he held his head
coming closer,
I felt grosser
but also had butterflies,
he couldn't look me in my eyes.
I licked my lips
and remembered the tips I'd been told:
'Don't stick your tongue in, you're only allowed to do that
when you're old.'
Suddenly we're toe to toe.
I breathed in and out, *Nice and slow*,
I thought.
'Sure you want to do this?'
I answered:
'I mean . . . it's only a kiss?'
Before I could say another word, he went in for the kill.
He moved his head a lot, and I kept mine still.
It was wet

really wet.

It didn't mention that on the internet.

He had a trail of snot leaking from his nose

that he usually wipes off with his clothes;

not this time,

it was now in our mouths, mostly mine.

The bell rang,

which was a lifeline.

I was getting bored.

Even though I was only young

the kiss felt like it verified my femininity.

All it took was losing my kissing virginity

to a boy . . . which was, of course,

not my first choice.

Unfortunately,

at that point,

my sexuality didn't have a voice.

I didn't really understand,

all I knew was that I'd much preferred

snogging the back

of my hand.

My battle with my own sexuality continued for many years. There wasn't an event or a moment that defined my sexuality during childhood, I just simply knew that I absolutely didn't want to kiss boys. I don't think I was brave enough or old enough to act on this knowledge. Other than dreaming of kissing women, I conformed to my gender role and got on with it. (Secondary school is where I went wild – we'll get there eventually.) The sooner we allow our children to understand that there are other sexualities, genders and identities that they can explore, the sooner we will make way for a more inclusive and accepting society. Thank you for coming to my TED Talk.

COUNCIL ESTATE OF MIND

So, when I wasn't lying through my back teeth in primary school, I was being good. Well, at least, I was trying to be. I liked it there. I liked the teachers, the food, the attention. I especially liked that my school at the time was only a stone's throw away from my gaff. It was ideal. I'd happily walk there and back on my billy tod every day.

It's strange, because council estates in general are viewed as very unsafe, unsanitary and unwelcome places, but that was never my experience of home. I think it's easy to have these views about working-class people and council estates from an outside perspective – if you're a small-minded bigot. I don't think it's harsh of me to say that, by the way; it's truthful. The saying 'don't hate what you don't understand' rings incredibly true. Just because a person's upbringing differs from yours, or they don't have as much money as you, or you have a porch and they don't, it doesn't ever give you the right to stick your nose up at anyone. I've felt safer walking through a council estate in the dark than I have walking through central London in the daylight. I never knew how judgemental people could be regarding your background until I grew up and moved to London. It's truly wild. People get off on hearing about your poverty growing up. The less you had, the more interesting you are. Safe to say, I am *extremely* interesting.

As a kid, life on the estate was all I ever knew. It's hard to put into words what it meant to me. The feeling of home was defined by so many unconventional things: knowing your neighbours like family; dancing at 3am to *Clubland Classix* with your mum; going river-walking on a hot day; the shopkeeper lending you a pint of milk until you can pay him back. The sense of community was endless. We didn't have a lot growing up, but what we did have was love.

I know you're still hung up on what river-walking is, so let me tell you. Mum would take us river-walking to really posh places like Bramhall Park. Basically, on boiling-hot days, we'd get a load of lilos for the kids and alcohol for the adults, then we'd take the dogs and just go and float and mess around in the muddy rivers. We'd dunk each other, and my brother would do front flips off the bridges. We'd be covered head to toe in mud and shit. Sometimes we'd make ropeys (that's short for rope swings) and swing into the water below. All the posh people that were there having sophisticated picnics would give us such dirty looks, which would ultimately encourage us to have more fun. My mum would say, 'Oh she's got a right stick up her arse. We're not hurting anyone.' We'd buy one of those disposable barbecues and cook up sausage butties until the sun went down. Just family, music and togetherness: that was all we needed to be happy.

Life wasn't all roses, obviously. We struggled, like every working-class family does. Mum had a couple of jobs and had bills to pay. She didn't always manage to pay those bills, which is understandable when you live under a government that doesn't want you to succeed – a government that wants to feed the rich and starve the poor. This never changes. I feel like this is a good moment to insert a poem. I hope you like it.

Council Estate of Mind

I'm going to begin by setting the scene: it's three-fifteen.
Primary school lessons come to an end.
I stand in the playground and wave off my friend.
Her mum picks her up and puts her in the car.
I swing my Morrison's bag home, it isn't too far.
I can hear kids laughing, and my shoes flapping,
I drew eyes on them today, looks like they're yapping.
My thumb twiddles through a damp hole in my sleeve,
which was my teacher's number-one pet peeve.
She'd say, 'Get ya thumb out of there,'
and I'd think, 'Shut up miss, I don't care.'
I walk through the back door, home sweet home.
I shout my mum but no reply –
It looks like I'm alone.
I open the fridge and hope for the best.
I'm greeted with out-of-date milk
and an open can of John West.

I take a dirty fork from the sink,
I dig into the tuna and I think,
'I'd love a McDonald's.'
I plonk myself on the sofa, with my tea
Just in time for *Tracy Beaker* on CBBC.
Half an hour in and the telly is no longer on,
I check the cupboard to discover the electric's gone.
'Shit.'

I pick the dirt from under my nails
as I scan the vacant room.
It's going to get dark soon.
Fuck this. I head out.
I knock on for a mate: 'You playing out?'
'Shall we play knock-a-door-run? Or shoot cars driving past with our
water gun?'
'Or we can make up dances, or write songs?'
On the front running riot, is where we belong.
We can talk about when we are older and we can buy booze,
as we stroll the streets without our shoes.
Soles of our feet are blacker than the night,
we leg it around the avenue to watch a playfight.

When I get in,
Mum screams:
'The bailiffs are at the door!!! Hide behind the sofa and lie on the floor!
Don't say a word, they'll soon fuck off.
The cheeky bastards want to take the lot.'
Round this estate you will never feel alone.
It's shite,
but it's what we know as home.
Everyone is skint but it doesn't matter,
'cause the times that are had are nothing less than mint.

The night fills with sounds of sirens and old-school garage blasting.
The echo of 'KIDS, GET IN THIS 'OUSE NOW' is everlasting.
We're rough, but we're always willing to lend a hand.
'Anything you need, love?' 'That'd be grand.'
The higher classes view us as nothing more than tracksuit-wearing scallys
that walk about with a Stella in one hand, in the other a Staffy.

They're puzzled by us, Rubik's Cube,
they view us as the other, spooky like *Scooby-Doo*.
They call us lunatics, like *Looney Tunes*
but we've got a survivor's state of mind.
Some have to turn to crime to pass the time and earn a few quid.
But don't be tight, he's not a bad lad, our kid.
Just doing what he's got to do
to get by.

I've obtained a first-class degree.
The only one in my family, and evidently,
I can speak more eloquently than you could ever dream to be.
I'm poor and raw and that's an unstoppable duo, can't you see?
I've made it this far without a penny off Mummy or Daddy.
Trust when I say it's all me.
But I'll never forget when I used to eat Oxo cubes for my tea.
There was nowt else in.

Cupboards were bare and we were painfully aware
as my mum would sit up all night on the kitchen chair in complete
despair, telling us:
'Don't worry kids, we aren't going anywhere,'
as she reread the eviction letters.
I was too young, so I never understood,
but I knew the bold red writing wasn't good.

Our government continue to raise the elite and shit on the poor.
We must riot and we must protest to prove to them
we're not having it no more.
Fuck the Tory government and fuck its law.
Enough is enough, if you want war, we'll give you war.
So down to earth we're engrained in it,
our feet stuck to the ground, we're chained to it.
This is us. And we're not ashamed of it.
Sometimes I feel discouraged,
I know I'm supposed to fly, supposed to flourish.
Give it time.

One thing about us is we love watching our own get to the top.
'She's working class her, from a council estate, the lot.'
So don't doubt that you can't do that as well.
You're gonna be a star, you are. I can tell.
But don't forget your roots when you make it.
We were dragged up, so we don't know how to quit.
I can tell you now, I won't lose the grit in my voice.
I'm a Mancunian, so I guess I've got no choice.
Council estate of mind,
we're rough around the edges.
But I'd say it's our number-one most perfect, imperfection.

There is a lot to unpack in that poem, and what better way to do that than through a nice word search puzzle; containing the stereotypical ideologies/words attached to council estates, usually assumed by middle-class people called Tobias who have zero idea what they're talking about. Enjoy x

COUNCIL ESTATE WORD SEARCH

W	D	E	G	O	A	T	E	R	U	P	T	O	S	V
A	R	T	N	T	U	O	W	V	F	I	V	P	C	U
R	O	T	W	N	C	H	A	V	E	R	F	C	R	H
V	A	R	Q	D	B	E	C	M	F	N	E	F	O	C
Z	C	A	U	S	I	L	G	H	S	S	U	O	U	H
K	V	C	S	A	S	L	I	O	U	T	A	T	N	O
Y	P	K	W	V	T	A	J	V	I	E	T	V	G	U
C	H	S	A	M	Q	B	R	N	L	L	G	I	E	S
O	L	U	K	Y	Q	P	E	O	Y	L	V	H	R	S
T	M	I	U	B	T	I	M	N	H	A	B	Z	U	G
A	H	T	H	U	G	S	C	H	E	O	R	S	L	Y
I	N	I	X	H	B	A	I	L	I	F	F	S	R	S
V	L	I	E	C	A	V	F	F	Q	O	I	P	U	A
Q	N	O	S	F	I	E	T	Y	S	U	E	T	O	J
B	N	C	V	U	O	S	S	H	P	W	U	W	S	P

TRACKSUIT
CHAV
STELLA
BAILIFFS
SCROUNGER
BENEFITS
THUGS
THIEF

Despite being poorly educated, benefits-scrounging, tracksuit-wearing thugs, do you know what we proper loved? Christmas. It was a big get-together. One year, it was due to be just me and Mum. She worked at the pub at the end of our road at the time. Everyone on the estate and in the village knew her. She invited everyone round to our gaff who didn't have anywhere to be for Christmas. So technically, the people that were spending Christmas alone were actually spending it with little me and my mum. I think there were eight of us in total. We lugged the tables from the pub and set them up in our living room. Mum cooked a massive dinner, and we all ate and played games together. There was a man there with long hair called Chris, and I specifically remember him setting the Christmas pudding on fire, and also his hand at the same time. He did it on purpose to make me laugh, even though it probably hurt. Everyone helped clean up, and they were so thankful. At the time, I remember looking around the table thinking, *Who the fuck are these group of randoms?* Now, when I think about it, it makes me feel so warm that my mum would do something as selfless as that. That's council estates for you: they're bursting with kindness (and thugs x).

ORAL HYGIENE

Christmas isn't *just* about being kind, it's also about getting presents. You would have seen my Argos page earlier, which I'd cover in circles for Santa. Santa usually got me what I wanted, as long as it wasn't too expensive – and was, of course, in stock. I imagine he'd jump down the chimney at Argos, holding my circled page, and just pick up everything I wanted. Get on this right, one year I asked Santa for a goldfish, and he replied with a little note: 'No goldfish in stock.' How out of order is that? All he had to do was just steal one from a pond somewhere; it wouldn't have even costed him any money, the tight git. Throwback to the days when Santa was real and made all of your dreams come true. Now, the thought of sitting on an old man's lap and telling him I've been a good girl this year makes me uncomfy. I'm glad I've grown out of that.

Anyway, Santa, aka Mum and Dad, never gave in to the goldfish idea. So, I had to take matters into my own hands. I went down to the local fair and won one playing 'hook-a-duck'. I brought it home in a little baggy and popped it in a plastic jug, on the bathroom window ledge. I called him/her/them Bob. I liked Bob. I'm not sure if I loved him, but I liked him. Unfortunately, he had a short and rather traumatic life. This one is called 'Plastic Jug'. Take it away, Soph . . .

Plastic Jug

Tuesday morning
I hopped out of bed and strolled to the bathroom,
yawning.
I grabbed my toothbrush from the side.
I squeezed on the Aquafresh.
Then the fish caught my eye.
I won it at a fair, Mum said I couldn't have it but . . .
It's still there.
I started to brush my teeth,
looking at Bob, and
I felt tight.
Nobody had ever brushed Bob's teeth . . .
And that wasn't right.
I was always told to brush my teeth twice a day,
so Bob's mouth must be full of decay.
I dipped my tiny hands into the tank,
scrambling to catch him,
his scales felt rank.
Gotcha.
'Now listen, Bob, I'm doing this for you. I bet your teeth smell like poo.'

I used my fingers to prop open his mouth.
My toothbrush explored his insides.
From north to south.

I felt proud.
I popped him back into his home.

He floated belly up, wasn't moving, didn't roam.
I think he must have died from shock syndrome.
Maybe he thought the toothpaste was too spicy?
Mum always said Colgate was too pricey.
Shit.
Maybe the bristles were too tough?
I was trying to be gentle,
I didn't mean to be rough.

I'd accidentally killed something
by trying to be nice.
I thought I was showing compassion,
for the first time in my life.

I can't believe what I did.
I felt so saddened.
I left the bathroom as if nothing happened.
I had to act shocked the next day,
knowing I was the one who took little Bob's life away.

What can we take away from me violently murdering my fish? Sometimes in life, when we think we're trying to help someone/something/a situation, we can actually be making it worse.

Moral of the story: don't worry about anyone else's oral hygiene but your own.

We're not even a quarter of the way in, and you already know the three most important things about me. I'm gay, I'm from a council estate and I'm a murderer. Joking: it was an accident, and I hope you haven't held it against me. I'm very regretful and remorseful, and if I think about it hard enough, I make myself cry. It was done out of love. Not violence.

I've been saving the best part of my childhood until last. I could write a thousand books on this, but I'll try and use my words to do this section justice.

LUKE

Luke is my nephew. My best friend, like a little brother to me. I found out I was going to be an auntie when I was seven years old. The prime of my childhood. Still a baby myself. I remember taking Stacey's pregnancy scan into primary school for Show and Tell – I got loads of attention. Me becoming an auntie was the talk of the school. I, of course, thrived on this.

Stace is nine years older than me. She's been like a second mum to me my entire life, which would naturally explain why Luke always felt like my little brother, rather than my nephew. Stacey has always treated me like her own, rather than her sister. She'd always buy me the best birthday and Christmas presents (that isn't the only reason I love her, but it was a definite perk). One year, she bought me a pair of real GHDs and some DKNY perfume. I was buzzin'. I'd join all of her family days out, holidays, weekends away; I really lived up to the stereotype of 'annoying little sister', but I think she enjoyed having me around.

There is only a year between Stacey and Matthew, so they had each other to play with, but by the time I was old enough to play, they were grown up and didn't want to any more. I actually think they found me *very* annoying. You know when your mum is really strict with her eldest kids, and then the youngest comes around and she decides to change her parenting style and chill the fuck out? I think that happened. Stacey and Matt reckon I didn't have it half as bad as they did when they were kids. I don't disagree; I think Mum mellowed with age, luckily for me. I don't blame them for finding me annoying. I used to lie to my mum to get them in trouble on purpose if they didn't let me get my own way. What a little shit I was. It would go something like this:

ME

Can I play with your make-up?

STACEY

No. Get out of my room.

ME

(starting to cry)

MUMMY, STACEY WON'T LET ME PLAY WITH HER
MAKE-UP!

MUM

STACEY, STOP FUCKIN' WINDING HER UP AND GIVE IT TO
HER, OR YOU WON'T BE GOING OUT LATER – AND I MEAN IT.

MATTHEW

She's such a little shit, isn't she?

ME

MUM, MATTHEW SAID I'M A LITTLE SHIT!

MUM

MATTHEW!!!!!!

ME

(laughs and sticks out tongue)

See what I mean? I would have disliked me, too.

So, when Luke was born, it was everything I'd ever wanted. Someone
I could play with, fight with, watch films with. Somebody I could grow up
with. I remember holding him in the hospital when he was born. I sat on
one of those blue, squeaky leather chairs they have in hospitals; my feet
were dangling above the floor. I wore hand-me-down K-Swiss trainers

from Gem across the road, and I had a grey hoodie on with my thumbs poking out of the sleeves. I was passed this tiny little blanket parcel, with a small human inside. I remember looking down at him and completely falling in love for the first time.

Luke and Stacey lived with us for a while when I was younger. Luke had a Spider-Man-themed bedroom; I loved it. When I used to wake up early in the morning, I'd sneak into his room and wake him up so we could play together.

I'm finding it difficult to try and talk about him, the things we did together and why he means so much to me. Really difficult. Almost as if my hands won't let me. They're sweating, and I can hear my heartbeat through my ears as I write this. So I'll do what I do best.

Luke

I remember taking Stacey's pregnancy picture into primary school,
to show all of my friends.
I was seven years old.
I was so excited to be an auntie to a little boy.
I'd struck gold.
I was a massive tomboy
so having Luke was like having a perfect little brother
to have playfights,
and Spider-Man nights.
When we'd play, he'd even take it in turns to be Mary Jane
so that I could be Spider-Man.
And that's where it all began.
His kindness as a child was heart-warming,
you couldn't not smile.
He went from playing with *Ben 10* and swords
to hoovers and ironing boards.
It was so sweet.
From the day that I held him after Stacey gave birth

he automatically became my most-loved person on this earth.
I just wanted him home,
I couldn't wait for him to become my bestest mate.
He had the most gorgeous blue eyes
that would go all sparkly when he was shy.
I have a fond memory of sleeping in bed with him
and Stacey when he was in nappies.
I never remember him crying as a baby.
He was always so happy.
He used to be obsessed with playing with hair.
It was a comfort thing
a bit like a teddy bear.
He slept in between me and Stace.
I'd always be hanging off the bed
with his little foot in my face.

He started to whinge, so I gave him my hair to hold
and covered him with the blanket
so that he wasn't cold.
He started to cry,
like he was unsatisfied with my hair.
It was strange.
So I exchanged
my hair with Stacey's
into his palm.
He started to snore.
He was calm.
He knew that my sister's hair felt different to mine
and that was fine.
I wasn't annoyed.
It was the moment I learned he was going to be
a mummy's boy.

When Luke was a toddler, he could never say, 'Sophie',
so he used to call me *'Rarash'* which is obviously
the next closest thing to Sophie. Supposedly.
I have an image of him in my head,
stood on the bed with his long vest and baggy nappy,
screaming *'RARASH'*,
it makes me so happy.
Once he had a small cut on his head
where he'd shaved his hair with my mum's Bic.
He never lived that down.
I always took the mick.

He would do anything that I asked him to
when he was younger.
'Luke, will you tickle my back?'
'Yeah.'
'While you're there, give it a crack.'
'Luke, will you get me a can of Dr Pepper?'
'Yeah.'
'Oh, and some cheese and toast. Extra Cheddar.'
Then, when he reached around eleven,
he'd still do it, but with an attitude.
A bit of aggression.
We'd have sleepovers most weekends, Friday to Sunday.
We'd watch films and play.
I always slept in Luke's room with him.
We used to stay up all night on *GTA*
after eating a takeaway.
Usually Chinese.
He'd always still be hungry.
'Can you go and get me a sausage roll, please?'
'Fine,' I'd say.
Luke used to sit down and watch me perform a cringe-worthy,

awfully bad dance routine.
I'd body-pop and sing in between.
It was truly horrific.
He'd act like I'd just performed the most terrific number he'd ever seen.
'Luke, what would you rate it out of ten?'
'Ten!'
'Really? Do you want to see it again?'
'Go on then,' he'd say with such excitement.
He never wanted to hurt my feelings.

He was incredibly sensitive and super positive.
Even as a fourteen-year-old teenager
you couldn't help but love him.
Blue eyes, cheeky smile and laughing always.
I picture that to get me through most days.
He had big, cute ears
that he was slowly growing into.
I'd say, *'You've got massive ears, you!'*
'I know I do,' he'd reply.

He sent me a text
six years ago,
saying:
'OMG, I'm growing a snail trail I am, I'm becoming a man!'
Even that was adorable.
We even used to sit and count his armpit hairs
until he grew into a hairy teddy bear.
Once he lost a dare
and had to wax his leg.
We cried laughing.

The thought used to cross my mind at least once a week.
That when I make it,

he'll be by my side.
Until the day I die.
He can have his own room in my mansion
and we'll never stop watching *Harry Potter* together
or wrestling outside
no matter what the weather.
Now the only time I feel him
is when I find a white feather.

Teens

I *must* start this section with something iconic that I feel sums up and introduces my teenage years appropriately. If you immediately get the words to this song stuck in your head, you're gay. I don't make the rules.

I am referring, of course, to the very classic 'All the Things She Said' by t.A.T.u, who, controversially, are apparently not lesbians. They could have fooled twelve-year-old me with their very raunchy music video – you all know the one I'm talking about. When they're outside in the rain, locked in cages, declaring their desires for one another. That music video was just one of my many gay awakenings. We'll delve into that later.

SECONDARY SCHOOL

Right, now that song is playing on repeat in your mind, let me set an important scene for you. Pay attention and cast your minds back. It's September 2007.

You slide into that brand-new, crisp uniform that's seven sizes too big. Your blazer is down past your bum and your shirt is itchy and stiff, the collar firm. Fresh out of the bag. Your tie is pristine, and you've done an alright job considering it's your first time putting one on. The length is key. Four stripes is too short, and five stripes is too gimpy. You manage a respectable four and a half. Your tights are soft and thick, no bobbles . . . yet. You've got some brand-new F&F Tesco school shoes.

They're giving you blisters, but it doesn't matter because they reek of that new, fake leather, and they're going to carry you through to at least 2009. You brush that side parting over as far as it'll go, and then you use half a bottle of Insette hairspray from Quality Save, making sure each strand is crispy and isn't going anywhere. You reach your little hand into your state-of-the-art Jane Norman bag and pull out a cold bottle of So . . .? Kiss Me. You begin to spray yourself from head to toe. You open your legs and spray your tights because . . . well . . . you never know. You smother your lips in a Cherry ChapStick and you give a single brush to your eyelashes with a dried-up Maybelline mascara that you found down the back of the sofa. You look at yourself long and hard in the mirror, before smiling modestly and leaving the gaff. Fleeing the nest. For your first day . . . of secondary school (cue dramatic music).

I feel like there is so much to dissect when it comes to school, especially for me. I know most kids can't wait to leave, but I was the total opposite. I dreaded leaving. In general, I hate change – most people do – and I couldn't fathom not having that routine any more. I never truly felt ready for that transition. School was a good place for me, overall. It was where I discovered who I truly was – and who I certainly wasn't . . .

PUBERTY
I was trying to think of a creative way to introduce puberty. So, I wrote a little scene. Use your imagination and let's get stuck in. Lights, camera, ACTION.

Elevator music plays softly in the background.

Puberty is a rite of passage. Scientifically, it is incredible, but we all know it's no fun along the way. From hormones to hair, spots to sex, be a fly on the wall for the most relatable date of all . . .

46

As Soph celebrates her twelfth birthday, she is given a very important envelope marked with bold letters: P.U.B.E.R.T.Y. This is Mother Nature's gift, and includes a save-the-date on the flip side – for Soph's date with puberty. She has heard her mum and a few of her friends mention puberty before, but she is completely clueless as to what it entails. This short takes on the format of speed dating. Instead of potential dates, Soph will find herself face to face with all of the elements of female puberty. Soph is unaware that she will be leaving the date with all of the elements, and is under the impression that she just has to pick one.

Each of the below will be played by me, as different caricatures introducing themselves to Soph (also me) for the first time:

BOOBS
Has enormous breasts, sounds flirtatious and loves Victoria's Secret.

BODY HAIR
Has OTT hair sticking out of multiple crevices, sounds mopey and is a vegan.

PERIODS/HORMONES
Is eating ice cream, sounds needy and always carries a full box of super-plus tampons.

SEX DRIVE
Has predatory eyes, sounds horny and keeps dry humping the chair.

ACNE
Has a huge under-the-skin spot and sits in silence throughout.

The piece will be incredibly quick-paced, cutting between different comedic moments between Soph and each caricature. I want the piece to crescendo as the dates become more intense. For example, Boobs will start by introducing herself politely, and will end by motorboating Soph. Sex Drive will start by giving Soph 'the eyes' and will end with thrusting on the table. Acne will remain silent throughout, and Soph will become increasingly awkward and confused as time passes with her. Both the caricatures and Soph will be performing to camera, to emulate the viewer being on the date.

Soph runs out on to the street.

SOPH
(to camera)

I can't pick, I don't want any of them, get me out of here.

All puberty caricatures rush to follow her. Soph legs it down the street, and the caricatures run after her.

HORMONES
(cries)

COME BACK!

BODY HAIR

We're all yours now.

BOOBS

I can't wait to grow on you!

SEX DRIVE

SEXXXXXXXXX.

ACNE SPOT

(bursts)

SOPH

(to camera)

I HAVE TO HAVE ALL OF THEM???

The comedic pay-off for this piece will be Soph running
away from the elements of Puberty, as they chase her into
the sunset.

Bows humbly. Thank you so much! I'd like to thank myself for going
through that, my mum for birthing me and my dad for helping.

ON THE BLOB

And that's pretty much how puberty works. The end! Kidding – I wish it
was. The worst part of puberty for me was starting my period. I remember
thinking, *What fresh hell is this?* I had it so awful. Worse than anyone else I
knew. I remember when it first started. I went to the toilet, looked down
and my knickers were covered in something brown. I automatically
assumed I was either dying or had shit myself. Much to my
disappointment, it wasn't the latter. So I must be dying. Twelve years old,
and this was the end. I hadn't even kissed a girl yet.

The first person I told was Stacey. She laughed. I cried, then she
laughed more. Naturally. We both told my dad, and he wanted to take me
to the hospital because he didn't understand why it was happening so
young, bless him. He's an over-worrier, by the way. Once I broke my wrist
in primary school and he drove to the hospital at about 80 miles an hour,
sweating profusely and beeping the horn as if I was at death's door. You'll
be happy to know I survived. If I so much as clear my throat on the phone
to him, he's like, 'RING THE DOCTOR. GO TO THE CHEMIST.' So
you can imagine his response when he found out his twelve-year-old had

starting bleeding and fainting. I think that might have been what caused his triple heart bypass . . .

I don't specifically remember having the conversation about my period with anyone prior to it happening. I mean, I'm sure my mum mentioned it, but I have no recollection. It was just thrown upon me, like a twenty-stone weight I had to carry around for pretty much the rest of my l i f e. My mum, my nanna and my auntie all suffered from bad periods; I think people say it can be hereditary. If that's the case, I was destined to be *fucked*. I remember one time I was at the George and Dragon pub with my mum, and she went to the toilet. So, I sat with my Diet Coke, thinking about going round to get a quid off all of her mates so I could buy some sweets from Leaders next door. She took *ages*, and I knew she didn't poo in public, so something was wrong. I headed into the toilets and the middle cubicle was closed. I sheepishly called out, 'Mum?'

She responded, 'I'm alright.'

I could tell from the tone of her voice that she was very much not alright. I looked under the cubicle door and saw a lot of blood, on the floor and in her jeans. She was trying to sort herself out, but there was no sorting *this* out. I cried because I didn't know what was happening, and I was scared for her. She eventually opened the door and told me it was 'adult problems', by which she meant something had burst inside her, some kind of haemorrhage, causing her to bleed, I learned later. And she bled a *lot*, although I don't think it was a matter of life and death. She told me what I needed to do to help: 'Run home and grab me a towel, a bin bag and a new pair of jeans.'

Mum obviously didn't want to cause a scene and let everyone know she was in a bit of bother. I was only young at the time, and it was dark outside. I remember being so scared, but I knew I had to do this for her. So I plucked up the courage to leave the pub, and start walking home in the dark. I had to go through this dark passage past the library, so I closed my eyes and ran as fast as I could through it. I realise now this method is flawed, because if someone was going to kidnap me, I wouldn't have seen them . . . Anyway, I went in the gaff, grabbed what Mum needed, and ran back. With my eyes closed.

She was alright, F Y I. We didn't tell anyone what had happened, though. It's one of those memories I still see so clearly; I remember exactly how I felt. How scared I was. How the pub smelled. It was back in the day when you could still smoke in pubs, so it smelled like stale cigarettes, beer and fear. Delicious. They should totally make it a perfume.

By the time I had started school, my periods were already *killing* me. The amount of times my dad had to come and pick me up from school – and I mean literally *pick me up*, because I couldn't stand – was unreal. It wasn't even the bleeding that bothered me that much, it was the *excruciating* pain. Words can't describe it.

I'm going to share a mega-embarrassing story now, one that only a select few people know. I'm not sure why I'm sharing it, but I feel like I should, to try and justify the pain to somebody who doesn't suffer this way.

So, I was staying across the road at Gemma's house, like I always did. Having a best friend that lives about ten metres from you is ideal. Me and Gem have been best friends since nursery; she is one of my favourite people on this planet. I was at Gem's house more than my own, so much so that I even used to stay there when she was out. I'd walk in the back door and Kay, her mum, would ask if I was staying for tea – which I always would. It was usually hotpot and dumplings. Then I'd go and get into bed with Kay, and stay up all night prank-calling people in her contacts list, and we'd cry laughing about it. I joined them on all of their family holidays and days out. Every Tuesday, we'd go to Morrisons with Kay, and we'd eat stuff going round the shop before dumping the packets. Nobody would blink twice if they saw me at Gem's; I was like part of the furniture. I loved it.

Anyway, that night, I woke up at around 4.30am with stomach ache. I went to the toilet to discover that *she* had arrived.

Ladies and gentlemen: *her*.

I panicked because I hadn't brought any painkillers with me, and I was usually at home when I came on, which meant I could suffer in peace. I started walking down their stairs and fainted with the pain. Before I fainted, my hands were shaking, I was dripping in sweat and my teeth were chattering. I mean, it *was* snowing outside – but these physical responses have always been a result of my period pain. Sometimes I also throw up 😖. I came around, and I managed to get up and get out of the back door. Everyone else was still asleep, by the way. I started slowly walking out of Gem's front gate, only to discover that all of the pavement and the road was completely covered with black ice. I couldn't even stand on it without going flying. So I sat down and dragged myself across the ice, on my arse, all the way to my house. I fainted again at my front door, and I was in so much pain that I couldn't even move to knock on. Then I felt it.

Shit.

No, literally: *shit.*

If you've ever felt period pain this severe, you'll know that you completely lose control of your bodily functions. So, as I lay there in the thick snow at 5am, thinking to myself, *It can't get worse than this* – it did. I shat myself.

In.

The.

Snow.

I don't recall what happened after that, but I remember waking up an hour later covered in snow and poo. I got the energy to bang on my door, and my mum came to the rescue. Imagine being in so much pain you fall asleep in the snow after shitting yourself and fainting *twice*. I'm sure you'll be thrilled to know that I was eventually (and when I say 'eventually', I mean fourteen years later) diagnosed with the ever-so-lovely endometriosis. #JustGirlyThings #LiveLaughLove #LadyPower.

So now you know that I have been haunted by my period pains pretty much my whole life, and I will continue to be. If you don't know what endometriosis is, google it. I'm sick of telling people. Also, some advice:

You'll be hairy, hungry, horny, and moody.
On top of that, you'll be incredibly broody.
They might say, 'You're being a bitch, are you on?'
In that case, hit them in the head with a yellow tampon.
That's important.
Don't waste the green ones –
they're *very* expensive and super absorbent.

So, what comes next in the realms of puberty? Oh yes!

BODY HAIR

I specifically remember finding my first hair. It was on my armpit, and I was so proud of it. I really looked after her, until she eventually fell out. RIP. Isn't it funny how, when we're young, we can't wait to go through puberty? And then when it actually happens, the whole thing is actual torture.

Especially for girls.

When I was in school, girls were absolutely not supposed to have any hair anywhere apart from on their heads, eyebrows and eyelashes. Anything other than that was 'disgusting' or 'weird' – so you can imagine my horror when I started to grow a bush. I remember watching my mum shave hers once, so I knew that was what you were supposed to do. (I didn't just go in and watch her, by the way; I was having a wee and she was in the bath. Every mum's dream – bath time disturbed by their child needing the toilet.)

So I waited until my next bath. That makes it sound like I rarely had one. I did – but we'd reuse the water. Mum would usually get in mine after I'd been in, so I needed to make sure that I didn't make a mess or she'd be suspicious.

I stepped out of my pants
and couldn't see the floor.
This mountain of hair

53

was all I saw.
Curly and black
from the front
through to the back.
It's getting out of hand.
So I picked up a razor,
Gillette was the brand.
I felt the sharpness of the blade
with my shaking hand.
It was my brother's, to shave his face.
If he knew where it was going
he'd be disgraced.
So I locked the bathroom door,
stepped into the water.
Legs on either side of the tub.
I got the soap
and I started to rub.
Bubbles masked my hair.
It's time.
I slowly glide the razor with care
upwards against the root.
I'm in pursuit of a smooth finish.
Time went slowly –
it had been five minutes.
I think the top is done?
Time to tackle underneath
through to my bum.
The internet said, *Be careful with the lips*
it'll bleed like a bitch.
And that, I soon discovered
as the razor uncovered
my first layer of skin.
Blood mixed with water created

this thin
murky red
as it bled and bled.
I thought
Shit.
I'm gonna have to tell my mum.
I'm gonna have to admit
to using Matthew's Gillette.
I jumped out of the bath with speed
and pressed on some toilet roll
to try and stop the bleed.
I glanced down
and was disappointed with my first attempt.
It was far from kempt.
Patches of hair, short to long.
I'd really fucked it up
I'd defo done it wrong.

I wish I knew then that body hair is beautiful.
It's natural for a woman, it's supposed to suit you.
Instead, I gave in to a societal expectation.
I shouldn't have to remove my hair to achieve self-justification.
Having body hair and being a woman
should have a positive correlation.
So let's end the negative stigmatisation.

I know you're wondering if my mum found out I used my brother's razor to shave my bush – yes, yes she did. The bathroom looked like a murder scene in a Stockport barber shop. I specifically say Stockport barber shop, because the windowsill was full of cheap candles from Poundland, and one of those signs that said 'Home is where the heart is'. (I personally felt the bathroom was a strange place to put such a sign. It should have said 'Home is where the shit is'.) Mum said I was too young to be doing that.

Too late, Mum! I felt like I'd activated true womanhood. I have to say, the novelty of shaving has most definitely worn off. I just forgot that Matthew will probably read this as well . . . Sorry, bro, but don't leave such a gorgeous Gillette razor lying about in a house full of women. You were asking for it. Mum used it, too. (Sorry, Mum.)

So, I was an early bloomer. By the time I was in year seven, I had my period, a bush and very little sore boobs. Emphasis on the little. Not much changed in the boobs department as I got older, sadly. These girls have been with me from the start. I think small boobs are in currently. I can't keep up with the trends.

I think I might have kissed a few boys? I can't really remember. I never remember the boys I've kissed, because they don't mean anything. The girls, however, I can't seem to ever get off my mind. Is that how straight people feel? Do you get butterflies when you remember the time you kissed a boy? I don't know how I'm expecting an answer . . . I'm going to google it.

OK, the first article that came up was: 'I feel butterflies when I see women kiss, but I feel nothing when I see straight couples. Am I gay?'

Babe, yes. Probably. I welcome you with open arms.

DON'T SHOOT THE MESSENGER

My dedication to being straight was admirable, truly. Do you *remember* MSN Messenger? Oh my god. I lived for it. Every day at school, there was some new form of MSN-related gossip. Or if you had something to say, it was always, 'I'll MSN you later.' Fancied someone? Get their MSN addy. Feeling upset? Post it on your MSN status. MSN in 2007–8 was like Instagram in 2021. It was essential, and anyone who didn't have an account was, quite frankly, uncool. I eventually grew out of making my relationship status apparent on MSN; even I couldn't keep up with myself. I did, however, enjoy logging in and out to let my crush know I was online.

I dated a boy at the start of year eight. For the sake of this book, I'm going to name him Blake. He was the first person I kind of . . . *liked*? I didn't love him, and I didn't fancy him, and I certainly didn't want to kiss him – but I didn't *mind* him. I could tolerate him, in small doses. Which was the furthest I'd got with a boy at this point. I made an MSN account shortly after. Throwback time.

Email address: Sophie4Blake4Eva@hotmail.co.uk.
MSN name: Sophi3 lOves Blak3 <3<3<3<3
Status: Blake my boy 4eva xxxxxxxxxx

He eventually dumped me, via MSN. The irony. This was the result:

Email address: Sophie4Blake4Eva@hotmail.co.uk.
MSN Name: Just Soph13 xxxxx </3</3</3</3
Status: Is listening to: Leona Lewis – 'Bleeding Love'

I feel like MSN is owed this one for being iconic:

Rushing home from school to talk to people you've just seen
From behind a massive 2007 computer screen.
You enter your details:
sexybaby303@hotmail.co.uk.
Password was your birthday.
Anxiously you wait for the log-in screen to load.
The two little green men circling, never gets old.
You're in.
It's a race against time to see who's online.
You spot your crush,
you think, *She's mine.*
One click and it's time
to prepare your opening.
You need to make her like you.

'Hi wuu2?'

Seventeen seconds pass, no response.

Jack pops up, oh what does he want?

'I wanted to hug u 2day, but u walked away:@'

Piss off, Jack. I should really tell him I'm gay.

One minute forty-two seconds later, a reply!

I'm nervous to open it.

OMG SHE SAID HI!

. . . .

'nuffin u?'

She absolutely likes me, I mean I always knew.

I'm going to take it to the next level and send an emoji.

I sent a tongue face :p and then accidentally a pony.

Fuckin' hell.

'Sorry dint mean tht'

'K'

'Wanna cum round to myn?'

NUDGE

WINK

Message declined.

'Biatchhuni27 went offline'

That's a true story. My ego was damaged, so I used a classic line in the manner of: 'Soz my friend wrote that', or 'OMG my dog stepped on my keyboard'.

LYING (PART TWO)

I feel like I need to be completely transparent with you here. You deserve to know that I hadn't grown out of my lying stage yet. If anything, I got worse.

I'm going to share a story that I'm not proud of, but at the same time proves that my dedication to the lie is BAFTA-worthy. I had bought a packet of stink bombs in a joke shop. For those of you that don't know what they are, the proof is in the pudding. They are *rotten*. A stink bomb is basically this yellow liquid inside a tiny glass vial, which you drop on the floor to smash. It releases the worst smell known to womankind. Imagine a combination of poo and eggs. Delightful. I, of course, carried a few in my pocket with the hope of getting out of a lesson, or causing commotion in the canteen. Anything for attention. But one day, I decided to take it one step further. I crept towards the office of my head of year at the time, slowly opened the door and stuck just my hand in. Then I threw the stink bomb, turned off the light and ran away.

During my sprint to escape the crime scene, I fell over. I mean, *proper* fell over. You know the kind of fall where it's anything but subtle? I smashed on to the ground in front of *everyone*. Luckily, I wasn't hurt physically, but emotionally I may as well have been dead. As I lay facedown on the floor, I could hear the gasps and 'Oh my gods' around me. Someone said, 'Is she OK?'

I was so incredibly embarrassed that I wasn't ready to get up off the floor. I needed a minute to just absorb what had happened, so I decided to play dead. Not *actually* dead, but passed out. It was the only thing I could do at the time to relieve myself from the horror of the situation. I was popular and cool, and this simply could not happen to me. Before I knew it, a teacher ran over to me and immediately put me in the recovery position. Fucking hell. She then tried to wake me up. Of course, I couldn't just wake up. I felt like I had started something here, and I believe in commitment. She ended up calling an ambulance for me. It wasn't until I was in the back of the ambulance that I 'woke up'. They reckoned that I'd knocked myself out in the fall. I agreed. I got the rest of the day off to 'rest' and see how I felt the next day.

I know what you're thinking. *Awful*, isn't it? I can't believe I wasted the paramedics' time and resources because I was too embarrassed to admit that I'd fallen over. I'd like to acknowledge that this isn't acceptable, and

I'm not proud of it – but can we at least admire my ability to see something through? I got so much attention that week, people being like, 'Are you OK?' Whereas if I'd just openly fallen over, it would have been, 'Ha ha, she fell over.' I did what I had to do.

I know you're wondering what happened with the stink-bomb situation. Later in the week, during my recovery, I was called into the office and shown black-and-white CCTV footage. It was me, very clearly me, throwing the stink bomb and running off. My response to that footage was, 'That couldn't have been me. I wasn't wearing black and white that day.'

I got excluded.

COOL DUDEY

I haven't stopped thinking about the fact that I referred to myself as 'popular and cool' during that last story. It's not sitting right with me, for some reason. Was it a big-headed thing to say? I don't think it's a *lie*. Maybe I just need to explain it a bit more.

Usually, being seen as 'cool' in school was because you were naughty and/or had a lot of friends. Both of those things applied to me. I think I overcompensated for the fact I was hiding my sexuality by being loud and disruptive. If my personality was huge enough to distract from and cover up everything else about me, I was winning. What would have happened if I had come out in school? What would everyone have thought of me? Would it have damaged my reputation?

I've always been an attention seeker, but I think in school I was an attention *needer*. The two are different. I think we need to replace the word 'seeker' with 'needer', because in my opinion and my experience, nine times out of ten, kids misbehave for a reason. Here are some of those reasons:

> They're not getting something at home.
> They're concealing a part of themselves.
> They're lacking confidence in other areas.

I think all three of those reasons applied to me. While I was busy being a little shit and entertaining everyone, I felt as though I was worthy, important and desired. For this reason, my relationships with my teachers were complex. I needed constant attention from them, and the only way to achieve that was to misbehave. It goes without saying, then, that not all of the attention was positive. In fact, it was mostly negative. But attention was attention; I'd take it. It was what I needed. It was a constant cycle of:

TEACHER

Why are you behaving like this? You're a clever girl with lots of potential.

ME

Not sure.

TEACHER

OK, well, don't do it again.

ME

OK.

ME

(does it again)

They'd always ask if something was going on at home. I never knew how to answer that question. We struggled at home with many things. Stacey and Luke had moved out when I was around ten, I think, and I missed them so much. Then there were issues with things like money, for example, and the fact I didn't like my mum's boyfriend. (I only liked maybe one or two of my mum's boyfriends; the rest were usually alcoholic arseholes who weren't very nice to my mum and took the piss out of her, basically. She wrongly paid more attention to them than me, most of the time, so I obviously resented them. One of her boyfriends used to send me to bed as soon as she went to work, even if it was the middle of the day. Evil.)

At the time, though, I didn't recognise or even create the space in my mind for that to be a reason I was misbehaving. My mum was preoccupied with other things, and I never spoke to my dad about any of my worries or issues. So, yes, I was lacking the attention that I so desperately needed. I think every kid that age needs attention, but when you're also trying to come to terms with your sexuality in a life full of poverty, it adds another layer of confusion and need.

TURKEY TWIZZLERS (PART TWO)

I just want to touch on poverty again before I move on. I explained how poverty had affected me in primary school: it *didn't*, massively, because when you're young, you don't understand the assumptions others may make about someone struggling with poverty, or the opinions they may have. I didn't really understand the eviction letters when I was a child; I just knew red writing wasn't a good sign.

But I was starting to understand a bit more about how it affected me when I started secondary school. I used to collect a dinner token from reception at the start of every lunch time. This was because my mum was earning below the minimum wage and essentially couldn't afford to give me dinner money. I remember being so embarrassed about collecting my token; I'd make sure that I went alone, and I'd only ever go and get it if nobody else was around. Numerous times I didn't collect it because there were people I knew close by. I think there were a lot of other kids in similar and probably less fortunate situations than me in school, but at that age it's not something you're open about, due to embarrassment and potential judgement from your peers. There was a hush-hush culture around it; it was like doing a dodgy deal with the dinner ladies when I handed over the token. The *worst* thing was when I'd ask for something and they'd reply with, 'SORRY, LOVE, THE TOKEN DOESN'T COVER THAT,' blasting it like a foghorn. I used to think, *Can you, respectfully, mind your fucking tone*. I'd feel my face going bright red and boiling hot as I scanned my surroundings to see who had heard.

I find that really upsetting now. I don't know why I felt so embarrassed. It shouldn't be embarrassing to be receiving help for any reason. I think, because I had upheld this reputation for so long of being funny, cool and put together, that I didn't want to risk anything tarnishing it for me.

I think people who are genuinely struggling are ashamed of needing help, whereas people that are doing alright don't mind asking for it. This is a small example, but I remember this lad in school asking people for a quid so he could get a cookie from the canteen. He wasn't embarrassed to ask for it, because he came from a decent family who had money to give him. I would never have had the confidence to ask something like that, because I was scared of being met with, 'OMG, are you poor or something?', or, 'Stop asking people for money, it's trampy.' So I learned quickly that it's usually the people who *don't* ask for help who need it the most. I've carried this ideology with me into adulthood. Those that have less will often give more, and I think that's down to generosity and community, which is something I experienced around me growing up. People would have next to nothing and still manage to help out those around them; it's just what we did. I like buying people drinks, even though I'm always in my overdraft. I want people to think I'm OK financially. When someone offers to buy me a drink, I panic because I don't want to say yes in case they think I'm a scav. Sad, really. So yes, if you see me in public in the future, just *buy* me the drink. Don't ask, or you'll embarrass me (happy with half a pint of whatever is cheapest, ta).

This one is called 'Turkey Twizzlers':

> Year five form a queue to the canteen.
> I jump around on the spot.
> It's my favourite:

smileys, fish fingers and beans.
It was always the same smell
you know the one.
I wolfed down every meal,
every bit of free food, gone.
Dinner lady Mrs Wright used to say,
'Good girl, now go and play.'
I had the energy for the day
to succeed, to work hard, to slay
from Monday through to Friday.
The best thing was
Mum didn't have to pay.
Parents all over the UK
knowing their kids will be eating today
meant more than they were able to say.
Some worked three jobs and still struggled, that's not OK.
But now we've reached a time where feeding hungry
children becomes debatable,
which, to me, is completely unexplainable.
Feeding a child is somehow now unattainable –
unfortunately, the funds are unavailable,
but a £3,000 pay rise for MPs was, somehow, favourable.
I'm not a red, I'm a blue,
but that doesn't matter when it comes to Rashford
campaigning from Essex to Trafford
Salford to Stafford,
showing us the way, to go against our leadership.
'If you can't feed your kids, don't have any.'
Get a fucking grip.
It seems the government can have a spending spree, restlessly, for
anything other than what's essentially one of the biggest horrors this
century, and eventually we'll have no choice. If we don't stand
up and use our voice.

Free school dinners allowed me to grow into the person I am today,
you can't argue with that. It's the facts.
I came home with some meat on my bones, and believe me,
I wasn't alone.
What we're doing just isn't enough.
'Can I have another fish finger please, Miss?'
'Course you can, love.'

DANNY

Anyway, where were we? Ah, yes. School. I pretty much had the same friendship group throughout the whole of school. One of those friends was Danny. He'd had a really similar upbringing to me, so we bonded instantly, and our sense of humour is worryingly alike. Our mums both liked to scrap, and we found common ground in our awful fashion sense, music and our love of taking the absolute piss. We were known as 'the troublemakers', both in and out of school. He's still one of my best mates now. If I told him I was feeling very down and wanted to unalive myself, he would reply with something like, 'I'll make sure you look snatched in your casket.'

And I love him for it.

VODDY IN THE PARK

I was a bit of a floater in school; I was able to hop from friendship group to friendship group, because, well, because I could. I got along with most people and would surround myself with different types of groups, depending on how I was feeling. Monday, what would it be? A good old swallow of my self-worth: a blow job in the park, and a black eye from a friend. How about Tuesday? Maybe finding comfort in my iPod Shuffle, making daisy chains and acting my age.

(Disclaimer – nothing wrong with giving blowjobs in the park. Just make sure it's what you both want to do, and that you're doing it safely with someone of the appropriate age.)

*

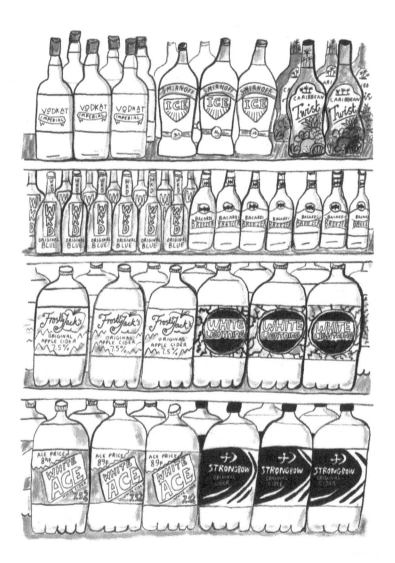

Everyone was dating, kissing, shagging everyone. We'd be out most weekends, drinking and causing trouble on the park. I remember one time, we'd bought cider into school before an exam. We poured it into an energy drink bottle and spun around on the school field, downing it in plain sight, before going into the bush to smoke a cig. I think it was before an English exam. Ironically, I got a B. Not too bad, if you ask me.

I'd stand outside the corner shop and ask someone to get us half a deck of B&H and three litres of White Lightning. I was a social smoker; the second a drop of alcohol touched my lips, I was all over a packet of menthols, although I never bought my own. I was a scav. I loved a drink though, probably too much for my age. Some of the classics I enjoyed were:

Frosty Jacks – the devil
White Lightning – the devil's sister
White Ace – the devil's mum
Strongbow – the devil's stepdad
Blue WKD – enjoyable
Vodkat – death
Cactus Jack's – sweet
Smirnoff Ice – gorgeous – still drink it now
Caribbean Twist – watered down
Bacardi Breezer – perfect on a summer evening

The list could really go on, but those were my favourites. I used to consume some of that selection at the age of thirteen. That sounds so young now when I think about it, but at the time, it was normal to me.

I once got so drunk at the age of thirteen that I ended up in hospital, and nearly had to have my stomach pumped. I completely blacked out, threw up and was genuinely unconscious (not pretending). I woke up to my mum at the side of the hospital bed, looking at me. I don't remember any of it because I woke up wasted, but apparently, I said the following:

> **ME**
>
> Where am I?
>
> **DOCTOR**
>
> In the hospital. I'm a doctor.
>
> **ME**
>
> Yeah, well, I'm a better one.
>
> **DOCTOR**
>
> How are you feeling?
>
> *ME*
>
> *(starts singing 'Hangover' by Taio Cruz)*
>
> **DOCTOR**
>
> OK. She's fine to go home.
>
> **ME**
>
> *(leaving)*
>
> Bye, everyone. Thank you, love you!

That was the only time in my life I was ever grounded, and my mum actually stuck to it. I was supposed to be going on my annual holiday with Gem and her family to Benidorm, and my mum didn't let me go. I was devastated. I remember looking out of my window, watching them put their suitcases in the car, crying my eyes out and listening to 'I'll Stand By You' by Girls Aloud. To make the scene even more dramatic, it was raining. I was supposed to be grounded for two weeks, but mum let me out after six days. She said I did her head in, which I did on purpose, as I knew she'd end up letting me out so she could have some peace.

That episode at the hospital didn't stop me from drinking, but it did allow me to realise my limit. As soon as the room starts spinning, I'll stop.

It's been sixteen years since that happened, and I can honestly say I've only been sick while drinking a handful of times, which I think is impressive. It all comes down to the fact I learned at a young age what can happen if you don't know when to stop: you'll be grounded and miss your holiday.

So, I continued to go out and drink and kiss boys I didn't want to kiss. I made my way around our whole friendship group; we all did. We were young, and it was exciting. I'd listen to my friends talk about the boys they fancied so much. Some of them were even in love. I obviously couldn't relate, but I continued to try *desperately* to fit in. I thought the more boys I kissed, the more chance I'd have of liking them.

Musical interlude no. 1: 2007

I haven't grown out of music from this era. Songs from 2007 absolutely bang, and I will not be told otherwise. Here is a brief interlude in which we can enjoy my top ten songs from that time, in no particular order. Please make some noise for:

'Bed' – J. Holiday
'Umbrella' – Rihanna
'Big Girls Don't Cry' – Fergie
'Like a Boy' – Ciara
'Cupid's Chokehold/Breakfast in America' – Gym Class Heroes
'Because Of You' – Ne-Yo
'Last Night' – Diddy feat. Keyshia Cole
'Ice Box' – Omarion
'Don't Matter' – Akon
'Heartbroken' – T2

And here are some non-musical but still iconic 2007 throwbacks:

- those shit plastic shutter glasses
- Myspace
- Bluetoothing songs
- that black-and-orange Sony Ericsson phone
- *Twilight*
- *Juno*
- recording your ringtone off the radio
- joining pointless social media groups ('Like if your name has a P in it')
- making your friends your sisters on Facebook

MY FANGIRL ERA

Between 2007 and 2008, my life changed forever. As I was exploring my sexuality, I was vulnerable and looking for guidance, and this led me to a stage every teen needs to experience: I was a diehard fangirl. Cast your minds back. It's November 2007. And after a 'Long Hot Summer', you're ready to 'Call the Shots' and go completely 'Out of Control'.

Sorry, that was so bad. I really wanted to create some sort of sexy riddle. A 'Sexy! No No No' riddle . . .

YES! You guessed correctly. It's Girls Aloud. Mainly Cheryl. But generally, Girls Aloud. I was absolutely mad for them. Truly obsessed. I'd be lying if I said I'd completely grown out of it, to be honest. I haven't. I still lose my shit in a club when their music is played.

I watched every performance they did, I went to every concert, and I bought every bit of merch – including their brand of Eylure eyelashes, which I never even took out of the box. I used to save every single penny my dad gave me, and I'd also pull the cushions off the sofa, trying to find any change that might have fallen down there – finders keepers, girlies! You couldn't even see the colour of my bedroom walls, because they were completely plastered in Girls Aloud posters, song lyrics and CD covers – the lot. Here's a picture for your viewing pleasure:

When I wasn't listening to Girls Aloud, I was thinking about them; when I wasn't actively thinking about them, I was still subconsciously singing their songs. I would even *dream* about them. Which makes me sound like a proper 'Stan' from that Eminem song, but I promise it wasn't *that* weird. I'm an obsessive person in general, so it was inevitable that I was going to become attached to someone/something eventually, and, *lesbehonest*, I was destined to fall in love with a girl group before I fell in love with a girl.

I remember the first time I saw them in concert. It was the Tangled Up Tour. Stacey took me, and I made a massive sign saying: 'I LOVE YOU SO MUCH CHERYL'. It's funny, because I was literally sitting in the gods, so Cheryl would have needed a telescope to see me and my sign – but I was, of course, convinced that she had waved at me. I cried my eyes out from the start of the concert to the end. It was a place I felt so happy; it was like heaven.

I joined a fangirl community on Facebook, a gorgeous little group called something like 'Girls Aloud Fans'. I had found my people. It was lovely, and a great distraction from my overwhelming and repressed sexual desires. For two years – no, genuinely – I used to proper tongue my posters. So much so that there were tiny, soggy holes where their lips were, and the paint behind the posters was started to degrade.

It was all sunshine – until they announced their hiatus, and my life came crashing down. I remember hearing the announcement of their break on the radio. I stormed out of my house and ran, screaming, down the street. I had a full-on breakdown. How funny is that? On my way back home, I was sulking and went to swing off a branch on a tree. The branch snapped, and I fell on the floor – which, ultimately, made me cry more. I'm honestly in tears of laughter writing this. The image of being that upset *and* falling over is *too* funny. How embarrassing.

Nobody panic; I survived. Cheryl took over from Sharon on *The X Factor*, so I was getting my Girls Aloud fix through her. Eventually, everything became about Cheryl. She was my new obsession. I think she always had been, really; Girls Aloud was just my only way to get to her.

I completely fell in love with her as a judge on *The X Factor*, but I also loved her solo music. I loved everything and anything she did. I changed my Facebook name to 'Soph Cheryl Galustian'. People had started calling me 'Chez' in school. I even got in a fight with someone who bad-mouthed her – like, an actual, physical fight . . . I got excluded, *again*.

I'd travel across the country to go and watch her, and eventually I met her so many times that she knew my name. Which – at that point – was my biggest achievement to date. I even had a huge group of 'Cheryl fans' friends who I'd met on the internet; one of them would become my girlfriend for six years. Crazy. Fast-forward thirteen years later, Cheryl follows me on Twitter and we have spoken regularly. She's helped me out with some of the biggest problems in my life, and she's given me the best advice. Twelve-year-old me would be *screaming* if she knew that. So yes, I do believe in the power of manifestation.

I feel like I should clarify that I no longer snog my posters. I snog real women instead. I did thankfully, grow out of that.

KISSING (PART TWO)

I kissed a girl for the first time in 2008. A *real* girl, not a piece of paper taped to my wall. It was a friend of mine, and it happened during a sleepover. As I've got older, I've discovered that this is really common. Obviously, it's different for me, because I am actually gay, but a lot of straight girls kissed other girls during sleepovers. They wanted to experiment, and I was *more* than happy to be that experiment at the time. We were lying in bed, just chatting, and there was a brief moment where I felt something that I hadn't felt before. That moment where you are looking at each other's lips, and you lean in, is almost as intense as the moment your lips actually touch. We kissed for a long time. A really long time. We'd sometimes stop and laugh in between, then carry on. The feeling I had that night told me everything I needed to know about myself. It was the feeling all of my friends had been talking about, twenty-four-seven. The butterflies, the shaking legs, the trembling lips. *This was it*. I'd just been kissing the wrong people (and inanimate objects).

We spoke about it afterwards and decided it was just a bit of fun. Which it was. All I knew was that I needed to have that feeling again. I craved it.

It happened at many more sleepovers after that, always with different girls. I don't know what it was. I never initiated anything, as I was always too scared, but it continued to just . . . *happen*? Maybe the girls had a strong gaydar and knew I was up for it; maybe they felt safe to experiment with me. Or maybe I just gave off a 'I want to kiss you' vibe. I honestly don't know. When I'd see the girls in school, we'd smile and look at the floor. Some of them avoided me altogether, because they feared it getting out. It was always a secret, of course; you couldn't be openly gay at my school without being bullied. You couldn't even admit to kissing the same sex without being hounded and labelled a 'dyke' or a 'lesbian'. I am trying to reclaim both of these words. I'm still working on it, though.

Our eyes locked
& everything else
disappeared

I closed my eyes
& tried to ignore
his beard

We were the only
two
people in the world

I desperately imagined
being this close
to a girl

Vision flicked from pupils
to lips

I felt too much
of his gripping fingertips

We edged in
equally
our lips met
and immediately

He began to kiss me
deceitfully

I felt whole

I'd given away
all control

Emotional, right? Grab the tissues. Every time I kissed a boy from that point on, it was getting more and more disappointing. As I got older, I encountered different sexual experiences with boys, which were even more disappointing. Even now, when I speak to my straight friends, they still find some of their sexual experiences with guys disappointing. So . . . I guess that's just some men in general . . . DO BETTER!

I was still trying to teach myself to like boys and trying to enjoy a more-than-friends relationship with one so that I could easily live my 'normal' life without being a lesbian. Eventually, people started to clock on. Obviously. It's really hard to conceal a part of yourself like that, especially when everyone around you is doing things that you don't want to do. It's like holding up a massive sign saying 'I'M A WEIRDO'. People would start asking me if I was a lesbian, which made my skin crawl. I couldn't stand being asked that question, because I was so ashamed, and I wanted to be anything *but* that. The more I was asked, the more the rumours would fly: 'Soph G is a lesbian,' 'Soph and so-and-so kissed at the weekend,' etc. My response usually went like this:

'EW, no?! What the actual fuck? That's disgusting. I don't know why you'd even ask me that, ah ha ha ha.'

This was that internalised homophobia I mentioned earlier. She's a real nasty bitch. I think this sense of shame came from my lack of knowledge about various sexualities, and also my disapproval of my own sexuality at the time. I just wanted to be 'normal', and because I felt unable to be, I ended up redirecting those negative feelings on to other people. If there was someone in the school who *was* openly gay (for the record, that would be maybe one or two people), I would join in with the whole, 'OMG, so-and-so has come out as a lesbian, ew.' I'm so sorry for that. I'm sorry to everyone I said that about or thought that about. I never meant any of it. I was doing it to get the attention off my own gay arse, which I know is beyond problematic.

I UNDERSTAND THIS MIGHT BE TRIGGERING FOR SOME PEOPLE WHO EXPERIENCED SIMILAR SITUATIONS, OR MAYBE FOR PEOPLE WHO AREN'T READY TO EXPLORE THEIR OWN SEXUALITY. SO HERE'S A BLANK SPACE FOR YOU TO WRITE DOWN ANY THOUGHTS YOU MAY OR MAY NOT HAVE AFTER READING THIS, OR YOU CAN USE IT TO DO WHAT I LIKE TO DO: DRAWING BOOBS.

All of this was so damaging to my 'coming out' process, and ultimately it caused me to do the complete opposite. I could no longer kiss *any* girls; I couldn't risk it getting out. Which meant I needed to find a new way to satisfy my concealed sexuality. Dun dun duuuuun . . .

WELCOME TO THE WORLD OF PORN

My god, where do I start with this one? My discovery of porn started in a very tame manner, but it went from Amanda Seyfried and Megan Fox in *Jennifer's Body* to 'MILF Gangbang' quite quickly. It should be noted that *Tom Jones voice* *it's not unusual* to be watching porn as a teenager. In fact, it's very common. Especially for female-identifying folk. That said, it was a lot more acceptable for boys to watch porn than girls. Like most things in life, it was OK for them and not for us. The boys would constantly joke about having a boner or having a wank, and they'd discuss what porn they'd watched. They'd send each other their favourite videos, or talk about who had shagged whose mum in it. Lovely. The idea that a girl could do the same thing was simply unimaginable. Much like the idea that girls don't poo. (Do you remember that shit? Pun intended.)

The mainstream videos did the job for a while. I'd rewatch my favourite ones so many times that I'd memorise every single thing about the video, from the breaths to the string of spit between their mouths. (I'm talking specifically about *Jennifer's Body* here.) It was all I had to hold on to, all I had to make me *feel* something. Eventually, these videos got boring, and no longer did anything for me. After rewatching the same three or four kissing clips probably over a hundred times, I needed to explore the internet more . . . (I also think it's hilarious that at this point, we didn't have Wi-Fi at my gaff, so I used to connect to Gem's across the road. Meaning I could only use my laptop when it was propped up on my windowsill. Basically, I had to hang out of my very double-glazed window. Sexy.)

I started off by watching videos on YouTube. I felt less shame that way, because YouTube is accessible to pretty much everyone, so surely whatever I was watching was OK. It was mainly short scenes from films. I obviously never watched the whole film. When someone mentions any film now with lesbians in it, I automatically know what they're talking about – but don't try and discuss the plot with me, because I honestly don't know what you're on about. I did try and watch *Blue is the Warmest Colour* in its entirety once; it was fucking boring. Nobody – and I mean *nobody* – watches that film for the plot.

Oh, come on, it was going to reach this point sooner or later. *This* really elevated my understanding of sex and sexuality. Probably not in the best way. I think it's generally felt that porn gives us a really unhealthy perspective on sex. Especially lesbian sex. We're taught that lesbians only exist through the male gaze – which, in simple terms, usually involves a heterosexual man sexually objectifying a woman for his own desires. It was almost impossible to find any videos that didn't involve a heterosexual man in some way, whether he was filming it, involved in it, or just watching the women in it. The women were dressed up to the nines, with six-inch heels, a full face of make-up and uncomfortably long acrylic nails. We all know what that means. It was all for show; it was there to be watched and admired by men. I had very little understanding of feminism at this point, but what I did know is that I felt contradicted. I was uneasy about how these women were being portrayed, but I was also thinking, *Wow, boobs.* Do you get me? It was clear to me at this point that lesbian porn was desired, admired and inspired by men. If that was the case, why was I made to feel so ashamed of my sexuality? Shouldn't the guys at school have thought it was cool that I was into girls? I understand how problematic that statement is now, but as a kid, that's genuinely what I used to think.

Once I was watching porn regularly, I started to feel more and more guilty. I don't know entirely what was causing this guilt. Was it that I was ashamed of my sexuality? Was it the fact that I shouldn't be watching it at all? I would almost instantly clear all of my browser history afterwards, and go on about my day as if it hadn't happened. But I felt dirty. Was I supposed to feel that way? I wasn't sure. All I knew was that I couldn't stop thinking about it – and I couldn't stop watching it.

It didn't stop at porn, BTW. Remember, this is 2008. And what was prominent during 2008, I hear you ask? Chatroulette. An online chat website that pairs random users for webcam-based 'conversations'. I use the word *conversations* lightly, unless you count 'ASL' as a convo-starter.

It was usually less to do with conversations, and more to do with harrowing visuals . . .

I think I used to go on Chatroulette because I was genuinely interested in what I'd see. Sometimes I was repulsed, and I'd close my laptop so quickly it would almost fly out of my window. Other times, I'd sit for hours, scrolling through to see what weirdness was going on.

It starts with sites like Chatroulette.
The camera opens . . . I break a sweat.
I can see, chest, lips & a headset.
'Hi baby girl, can I make you wet?'
CLOSE. Clear history.
I was hoping 'he' was a 'she' . . .
It had me thinking, *That world is a mystery.*

So, I open Google
And I search *'sex'*, hesitantly.
Results stand at 204,567,283.
'Should he wear a condom?'
'My penis is 3 inches, is that a problem?'
'Do we need it?'
'Anal, blow job, massive arse, fake tits'
'Sexuality fantasies'
'Orgies with twos, or threes'
The options were endless.
'Pornhub' & *'RedTube'*
'Ladyboy, squirting, long pubes'
I was overwhelmed.
I clicked on the first one that caught my attention.
I sat in complete suspension as the video opened.
I remember the first words that were spoken:

'I've been a very bad girl,'
a young woman said as she gave the teacher a twirl.
My pupils grew as the women groped and kissed each other.
Before I know it, it was finished.
So, I searched for another . . .

My ban on kissing girls (to misdirect any rumours of me being gay) didn't last that long, FYI. If anything, the porn just made me want to kiss girls more than ever. At least now I had something to imagine when I was kissing boys; I would imagine they were girls. (I should mention I use the word 'kissing' lightly. In this book, kissing can mean anything from actually kissing to shagging. Use your imagination – and no, when I'm talking about boys now, I don't mean shagging.)

My repressed sexuality was just starting to leak out in other ways. We're about to dive into 2009. *The* haircut. But just before that, a short reminisce on the best songs of 2008.

Musical interlude no. 2: 2008

'I Kissed a Girl' – Katy Perry

'Heartbreaker' – will.i.am feat. Cheryl

'Fascination' – Alpha Beat

'No Air' – Jordin Sparks feat. Chris Brown

'Closer' – Ne-Yo

'Forever' – Chris Brown

'Superstar' – Lupe Fiasco

'Live Your Life' – T.I. feat. Rihanna

'All I Ever Wanted' – Basshunter

'What's it Gonna Be' – H 'Two' O feat. Platnum

Other iconic things from 2008:

- Apple Bottoms jeans
- boots with the fur
- poking on Facebook
- 'like for a rate'
- neon-coloured plastic pearls
- knee-high socks
- vest tops
- Tumblr
- *The X Factor*
- that time David pushed Gail Platt down the stairs in *Corrie*

QUEER VOCAB

I'm going to introduce this section with a nice 'lesbian key identities'
word search. Enjoy:

LESBIAN WORD SEARCH

S	W	A	E	M	E	L	O	M	K	E	F	D	M	O
C	P	W	O	P	P	K	Z	C	B	E	Q	Y	F	G
H	U	I	Q	U	B	D	A	U	V	M	O	K	U	D
Z	R	F	L	D	G	Y	E	F	E	M	M	E	E	C
S	T	I	C	L	H	R	U	S	D	H	I	J	M	H
B	C	H	E	I	O	P	U	B	Y	M	K	S	G	A
J	X	I	L	P	E	W	E	H	U	C	A	S	I	P
Q	J	U	L	S	X	O	P	O	L	T	O	P	T	S
C	S	S	O	T	A	Q	P	R	M	S	C	T	U	T
R	T	U	W	I	Y	J	S	U	I	S	D	H	B	I
E	U	E	T	C	K	Z	T	O	N	N	O	D	Z	C
M	D	M	P	K	O	U	R	U	T	O	C	Y	A	K
E	I	M	O	H	P	Q	O	S	U	P	M	E	N	E
J	Q	O	G	S	T	E	M	M	A	E	O	T	S	T
O	T	W	Y	L	V	P	W	R	U	N	S	M	X	S

PILLOW PRINCESS
LIPSTICK
FEMME
DYKE
STUD
BUTCH
STEM
CHAPSTICK

If you don't know what the words mean, allow me to explain them to
you. I must note, these are mainly my opinions and a bit of Gay Twitter
knowledge. These are *not* facts. It's also totally OK if you don't
identify with any of the below. Not everyone does.

> **Femme:** girly girl, couldn't possibly be a lesbian because she wears make-up
> and looks like a . . . girl.
> **Example:** Dani from *The L Word: Generation Q* – fictional character,
> desirable bad bitch.

Lipstick: Known to be the most femme kind of our species. Will wear
a dress and has no issue walking in heels.
Example: Sarah Paulson – a brilliant actor and an iconic gay.

Butch/Stud: Often accused of wanting to be men; great at challenging
the social norms of how women are 'supposed' to look.
Example: Big Boo from *Orange is the New Black* – fictional character,
a legend among many.

Stem: A bit of a tomboy who wears make-up, pretty much. Somewhere
between a stud and a femme.
Example: Samira Wiley.

Pillow Princess: a high-maintenance gal who loves to be the receiver
of sex; probably has acrylic nails.
Example: A straight girl.

Dyke: Historically, a derogatory term used to describe lesbians.
Now reclaimed and used by us.
Example: Anyone who's comfortable being called one.

I usually refer to myself as queer these days. It's easier. I sometimes call
myself a dyke in front of straight people as it makes them feel
uncomfortable, which is *always* fun.

THE HAIRCUT

So that summer, over the school holidays, I decided to switch up my style a bit. I don't know why I did this; I think it was an impulse, and maybe a not-so-subtle attempt to lean into my gay truth? Before this, I'd had plain, long, brown hair, and I didn't really wear make-up, unless you count a Cherry ChapStick. (Katy Perry outed me.)

Bearing in mind I was totally obsessed with Girls Aloud, I was trying to figure out which of their styles I should copy for myself. That's what happens when you're obsessed with someone. You either want to be them, or be *in* them . . . or, in my case, both. At this time, my mum had been cutting my hair with nail scissors for the last four years, because going to the hairdresser cost an arm and a leg. But my dad said he would get me a haircut as a birthday present. He was good like that. So, I cut out a photo (with those very nail scissors, ironically) of the gorgeous Sarah Harding's bleach-blonde pixie cut of 2008. Brave, right? I took that photo to the hairdresser and quite simply said, 'I'd like this, please'. My mum was unsure, but, true to her style, let me do whatever I wanted. She just said that if I regretted it, I'd 'only have myself to blame'. Cheers, Mum.

The hairdresser was like, 'Are you sure? It's a big change.'

I said, 'Listen, Trisha, chop the fuckin' lot off. I *need* a change.'

I didn't really say that. But you get my gist.

Oh, I forgot to mention. I also asked her to dye it bright red – so tell Rihanna *I* did it first. Can you *believe* that while trying to hide my sexuality, I thought it was a good idea to get the biggest dyke haircut on the *fucking* planet? I may as well have had 'MASSIVE LESBO' tattooed across my forehead. I remember looking in the mirror afterwards, thinking, *What the fuck have you done?*

This is a great example of how impulsive I am; if I think for a split second that something could be a good idea, I'll just do it. Regardless of the consequences. Which is probably why I *always* seem to find myself in some sort of trouble. Of course, I did the classic thing that everyone does when they get their hair cut, when the hairdresser says, 'Do you like it?'

and you respond with, 'I *love* it,' even though you now want to chop your own head off 😵.

I remember going back to school after the holidays and people not recognising me. Everyone seemed to love it at the time. It was fashionable. If I did it now, I'd look like a Karen, and *nobody* would want that. I used to style it with Dax Wax, and once I put a Facebook status up with the following:

Hmm . . . Hair Spiky Or Flat 2morra? Xxx

This just *screams* dyke. People started calling me 'Red 'Ed', which I obviously loved, because it was essentially more attention for me. I eventually changed my Facebook name to 'Soph Cheryl Red 'Ed Galustian'. I needed everyone to know that I was the girl with the bright red hair. I think I was in school for approximately three days before I got sent home because of the colour of my hair. The head teacher at the time called me into his office and expressed his 'disappointment'. He described my hair colour as 'distracting' and 'unnecessary'. I, of course, was being a gobshite and answering back – rightly so, in my opinion. I've never understood why kids get sent home for expressing themselves. Whether it's make-up, a haircut, piercings, shoes – I don't see how that affects their learning? If anything, individuality should be encouraged, not repressed. I'd just changed my appearance in the hope of changing myself. I don't think teachers always consider *why* people are altering their appearances. It isn't always just for fashion or attention; some kids do it to escape themselves or distract people from other elements of them. I went home and told my mum everything that had been said to me. She went mad. She was never very good at articulating her disapproval without shouting, so we got my brother-in-law, Alex, to write a fancy letter for me to give to the head.

Dear Mr Mind-Your-Own-Business,

I am writing to you to express my deep disappointment in relation to your comments about my daughter's hair colour. Sophie is and has always been a very expressive character, and I cannot fathom how she is being targeted due to her individuality – which, I might add, is highly encouraged at home. Am I right to assume that you have an issue with every student who has not maintained their natural hair colour? If that's the case, I imagine you've stopped many students from learning. As a head teacher, this shouldn't be the case. Why don't you focus on attempting to run your school, and I will continue to not only condone but embolden my daughters' choices. If you have an issue with any of the above, you can call me on ***********.

Regards,
Clare

MIC DROP. Go on, Mum! Well, go on, Alex! The head didn't say anything to me again, and I didn't have to change my hair colour. A few of the jobsworth teachers would say to me, 'Are you allowed that hair colour?', and I'd always respond with, 'Yeah. My mum's spoken to the head.' Those teachers would then be embarrassed. Rightly so. Focus on teaching me and stop getting involved in my lesbian appearance crisis. I'm under enough pressure as it is.

FIGHT FOR THIS LOVE

Everything changed for me in 2009. Not only was it the year that I got a shit haircut, but it was also the year that I genuinely fell in love for the first time. When I think about kids in year nine now, I automatically think how young and inexperienced they must be – until I think about myself at that age, and I know that I knew way too much by then. I had to grow up young, and 2009 was the year that *really* started to happen.

First things first: this was the year that Cheryl released 'Fight for This Love'.

I remember I stayed at Stacey's that night. She had a little flat in Gatley, and was heavily pregnant with my beautiful niece, Ems. I was in their computer room at the time, waiting for Chris Moyles to give 'Fight for This Love' it's debut play on Radio 1. I was in tears because I was so excited. I remember Luke coming into the room to listen to it with me. At that age, he always took an interest in whatever I was into; I guess he thought it was cool. Such a sweetheart.

It was 7 September 2009. The strings came in, and Chris followed them with: 'It's Cheryl Cole's new song, "Fight for This Love".'

I was honestly levitating. Or what felt like levitating. I absolutely could not get enough of it. I remember Luke saying, 'Do you have to listen to it *again*?'

The answer was yes.

I think Luke is what makes that memory so special. I recall it being a school night that I stayed over at Stacey's, which was my absolute *favourite* thing. She'd always get us a Chinese takeaway and we'd go to Blockbusters to get a film (throwback). She'd wash all of my uniform for me with softener, and then put it in the dryer in the morning so it was warm. She was the only person I knew with a dryer. Drying clothes in a dryer is a game changer. It makes them smell and feel *so* good. I was used to hanging my clothes over an ice-cold radiator due to having no electric. Everything would stink of damp and feel rough and crusty, and I've always had a thing about smells. I like to smell nice all the time – which, under the circumstances, was difficult at home. Stacey's dryer had the opposite effect of the radiators at home.

She also always had so much good food in. Luke was seven at the time, so needed packed lunches, and that meant Stacey had all the best things in the cupboard. Crisps, biscuits, sandwich stuff. Even cans of Coke! I'd stuff my bag when I was there. It was a real luxury.

I'd get up in the morning, have a nice warm shower, and dry myself with a proper thick towel that smelled of fresh washing. Not one of those crusty, dusty Primark ones; it was like a John Lewis towel. Then I'd go and use Stacey's moisturiser and make-up. I'd even use her hair products for my shit hair. Lastly, I'd spray her perfume. DKNY in the long bottle: it'll *always* remind me of her. I'd put on my fresh, warm uniform and eat breakfast with Luke. I *never* ate breakfast at home. Actually, I did sometimes; I used to eat the Bombay mix from last night's curry in the morning. It was alright, to be honest, but I didn't always want to go into school smelling like turmeric and damp.

I know all of that might seem so simple, but it made a huge difference to how I felt about myself. For example, after having my uniform washed like that, I'd go into school and feel *so* good. Fresh and warm and ready for the day. I'd spend whole lessons sniffing my jumper and feeling my soft, clean skin. When I think of Stacey, that's what I feel. I feel like she's my home – always has been, and always will be. She provided relief and comfort when I needed it the most.

After that morning at Stacey's, I listened to 'Fight for This Love' *so* much that I convinced my dad to buy me one of those tiny little iPods without the screen, I think it was called a Shuffle. 'Fight for This Love' was the first song I illegally downloaded on there. Those were the days when you'd do an MP3 conversion of a YouTube link to get your music. I have to say, it was an upgrade from Bluetoothing songs or recording your own ringtone. I took that shitty little Shuffle everywhere with me, with that one song on it. There was nothing in the song I could really relate to at this point; I'd had no major traumas or heartbreaks. These days, I overplay songs because they remind me of someone or something. I usually do it because it hurts, and I want to feel something. But I didn't have the pain of that yet; I didn't have the pain of memories. Just the ability to simply enjoy a song.

HERE'S ANOTHER BLANK PAGE YOU CAN USE FOR
REFLECTION. MAYBE WRITE DOWN THE FIRST SONG
YOU EVER LOVED. OR A SONG THAT REMINDS YOU
OF SOMETHING. A PLACE, A SMELL. ANYTHING.
OR, AGAIN, DRAW SOMETHING MEANINGLESS.
YOUR CHOICE.

REBEL

So, by 2009, I'd established myself as a rule-breaker at school. Not only did I throw stink bombs around the gaff, get into fights and have bright red hair, but now I walked around with earphones in, listening to my new favourite song, as if none of the rules applied to me. My excessive drinking and occasional smoking had increased dramatically. I was going through that proper teenager stage where everything is heightened, and you fucking can't get enough of it. I was rebelling, big time. I'd kissed every boy in our friendship group, and was well and truly bored. My sexuality was, as always, repressed. Even if my hair said otherwise.

The teachers started to clock on to what we were up to at the weekends. Drinking, fighting, smoking and shagging. I remember getting called into a meeting with one of the department heads at the time. She scared me, but I actually really liked her. For the sake of this book, I'm going to call her Miss Mooney. She'd take me out of the most boring lessons, like Maths, and bring me to her office. It always smelled like coffee in there, but the chairs were super comfy. The kind of chairs that you melted into; once you'd got comfy, it was impossible to get out of them. She'd talk to me like a friend would, asking what I was up to at the weekend, and who I enjoyed going out with. I might have been young, but I certainly wasn't stupid. She was trying to get me to grass on myself and my mates for breaking the law every weekend. Technically, she couldn't do anything about it, because we weren't on school grounds. It was literally the weekend, so I wasn't sure at the time why she was so interested. I can understand now that she was a welfare teacher, so naturally wanted to know if we were putting ourselves in danger. Which, of course, we really were.

I always liked the female teachers that were a bit scary. I don't know if it was the authority or the fact that it showed how much they cared, but I have always gravitated towards female teachers that told me off. As an adult, I recognise that is now called 'having mummy issues', but at the time, I was blissfully unaware and just thought that I, strangely, enjoyed being in trouble with sexy older women.

Anyway, Miss Mooney soon figured out what my friends and I were up to, and she referred me to a mentoring programme called Mosaic. This was a local charity that focused on 'creating opportunities for young people growing up in our most deprived communities' 😊. That's me! Woo hoo! I would go there once a week with a few of my close friends at the time to talk about what we got up to at the weekend. It was fun, because we were completely honest, and we found the whole thing amusing. We went on to complete a course in alcohol safety at the tender age of fourteen, and received a certificate upon completion, which I stuck on my wall among Cheryl and Girls Aloud. I'm sorry to inform you that it didn't stop me from drinking. However, it got me out of lessons for an hour, and for that, I am grateful.

By this point, the partying was getting a bit out of hand, and my constant battle to conceal myself was putting me in dangerous situations. I think, in hindsight, that the charity intervention could have been useful if I'd taken it more seriously. On reflection, I wish I had done, but in true me-style, I didn't. Instead, I actually ended up getting myself into worse situations. I mentioned earlier the annual holidays I went on with Gem and her family. I honestly lived for them. They were the best. We'd started by going to Tenerife, then we moved on to Benidorm. That was my first proper 'girls' holiday – even though I was only fourteen, Gemma and I went off and did our own thing. They don't ID you in a place like Benidorm; we got into every bar and club we wanted. Most of the time, we were physically picked up by the reps outside and carried in for a free shot. I felt like such an adult. One night, we had a lock-in at the club with these two Spanish guys. I reckon they were in their late twenties. We probably lied about our age. I certainly didn't *look* fourteen. At around 5am, when the sun was coming up, we went down to the beach to skinny-dip. Then we went back to the hotel, had breakfast, and carried on drinking. If I even attempted to do that now, I'd end up hospitalised. I can't hack it anymore, probably because I overdid it when I was too young.

*

If you hadn't guessed by now, I enjoy overindulging in iconic reality TV, so please enjoy one of my favourite TV moments from *Bigg Boss*, the Indian version of Big *Brother*:

POOJA

(kicks dustbin by mistake)

SHONALI

Pooja, what is this behaviour?

POOJA

I'm sorry. I kicked it by mistake.

SHONALI

You can't kick it by mistake!

POOJA

Then pick it up if it bothers you!

SHONALI

No, you pick it up.

POOJA

You don't tell me what to do!

SHONALI

I can tell you what to do.

POOJA

You don't tell me what to do!!

SHONALI

Dustbin—

93

POOJA

You don't tell me what to do!!!

SHONALI

Or what? Are you going to hit me?

POOJA

Do you want it?

SHONALI

I don't . . .

POOJA

But you're asking for it, you're dying for it! GET. OFF. MY. BACK.
Got it?

JULY (PART ONE)

For me, being a teenager was about being optimistic. You're waiting to finish school so your life can officially begin. We spent so much time envisioning possibility and prosperity that, in a way, we let the most important years of our lives slip right past us. That's how I feel now, anyway. Let's get back into 2009.

So, I'm back to school after the summer. It was a good summer, for the most part. I'd illegally downloaded hundreds of new songs on to my Shuffle via Gemma's Wi-Fi, and my hair had started to grow on me, *slowly* but surely. Something was still missing, though. Of course it was. It felt like everyone around me was in a relationship. I know that shouldn't have been my main focus at my young age, but I couldn't help feeling *different*. This is probably what led me to fall in love. For the sake of this book, I'm going to call the person I fell in love with July. July was my first love. She was *everything to* me. She taught me love, and with love always comes pain. So she taught me that, too.

July and I first made friends after Sports Day, which was always a fun day. It was a day you could wear your PE kit and piss about with your mates, basically. I'd seen July run the hundred metres rather quickly, and I was impressed. So, I made the first move and posted on her Facebook wall – innocently, I might add:

Wow, you're such a fast runner! I saw you and I was like :O :O! xxxx

We became friends after that. Just like my other friends; nothing different. I had a lot of friends. I use the word 'friends' lightly. I just knew a lot of people, because I was a gobshite and made sure everyone knew it. But July and I soon became best friends, inseparable. This was around the time BlackBerry phones were in fashion, so we would be on BBM (Blackberry Messenger) from morning until night. When we were together, we'd change our BBM statuses to 'July with Soph :P' or 'Soph – chillin' with July'. I acknowledge I hadn't completely grown out of my MSN phase, OK?

We eventually had our first sleepover, which was so exciting. We'd planned what scary films we were going to watch in the hope we'd do an all-nighter, because for some reason, when you're a teenager, it's cool to stay up all night. I couldn't think of anything worse now. I need at least nine hours to function.

So, I was at her house and she had her tea. I said I didn't want anything. I was doing that classic thing where I was hungry, but I didn't want anyone to know, so I convinced her and her mum that I'd already eaten. This was because I didn't have any food at home and was embarrassed, and also because I wanted to be delicate and ladylike, which obviously meant I wasn't allowed to eat or use the toilet, as that would ruin the illusion. Hilarious.

We stayed up so late. We watched the shittest horror films; she was never scared. But I remember my palms sweating because I was terrified. I've never enjoyed horror films. I was exposed to them too young as a kid. Once Matthew was babysitting me, against his will, and he put on one of the *Saw* films and then fell asleep. I needed a wee *so* bad, but I was too scared to move, let alone go upstairs to the toilet, so I literally pissed myself on the sofa. Luckily, it was a leather sofa that was a hand-me-down; it had had its day. A wee brightened it up a bit, I think. It's not as bad as the poo in the snow, but embarrassing, nevertheless.

I didn't tell July this. I was hoping I'd be over it. After we'd watched two or three horror films, we lay down in bed, face to face, talking all sorts of rubbish. It's so funny, because I can barely remember what I did yesterday, but I remember every single detail from that night. The smell of her room was the same smell as her school uniform: fresh washing and the smell of her skin. I remember what colour her bedsheets were – shiny black – and the tiny bit of moonlight that peeped through her curtains as we laughed together. We shared so much that night. I remember instantly feeling close to her, like I'd known her my entire life. That's the only way I can describe it.

And then it happened. We kissed. So naturally. We kissed all night, for what felt like hours and hours. We kissed until the sun came up and our eyes were squinting from the light. I felt as though our hands had touched nearly every inch of each other. I know I've been here before, with kissing at sleepovers, but this, for a reason I didn't know at the time, felt *so* different. I mean, it *was* different. The kisses before had felt like fun; this was deeper than that. We slept for a few hours, and when we woke up, we just stared at one another. She was half hiding under the quilt. She did this a lot. I could just see her eyes. I was smiling, and then we started laughing. We kissed again. This hadn't happened before; the morning was always completely different, tinged with embarrassment. But with July, it wasn't. It all came together, for the first time. I didn't want to leave, but I remember I had plans for the evening. I wanted to cancel every plan I had and just stay there, in bed with her, forever. Everything felt so right.

This might seem full-on for some people, but you have to remember, I was deeply repressing my sexuality, and for the first time in my life, I'd felt like I'd been opened up and accepted by someone. July had given me something I'd been craving for so many years. We hugged, so tightly, and when I left, she stood at the door and watched me walk down the road.

I had a spring in my step. I got out my Shuffle and popped on 'Disturbia' by Rihanna: an interesting choice, I know, but it was my jam at the time. I walked to the closest shop because I was literally shaking with hunger. I got myself a packet of Skittles and an energy drink, then jumped on the number 11 bus home. I remember that bus journey so well. I was going over every single detail of the night in my head; so much so that I missed my stop and had to walk back. I was beaming from the inside out.

I got home and Mum asked if I'd had a fun time. I, of course, said yes. Then I ran upstairs to get on BBM and message her. We just both said we'd had a nice time; we didn't discuss anything in detail or even mention the kissing. But we were flirting, so that was good. I remember not wanting to get in the bath because I didn't want to wash away the night.

After that night, I think I stayed at July's every single weekend. I sometimes stayed on a school night, and her mum would drop us at school the next day. We were working our way through every horror film available on 123Movies, as well as discussing our favourite songs. We'd listen to them all on YouTube and kiss until the sun came up. We told each other absolutely everything, every secret, every thought. I didn't understand how I could spend so much time kissing one person and not get bored. Five hours with her felt like five minutes; I could *never* get enough. It was perfect. She was perfect. I finally had everything I'd dreamed of for so long. I made her laugh. A lot. I loved this. I've always loved making people laugh; I'm good at it. The very little time we spent apart, we were texting, and when we weren't texting, I was busy thinking about her. I remember the first time she told me she loved me. We'd said it before over text, a lot. But in person was different. She just said, 'I love you, Soph,' and of course I said it back. I did love her. I hadn't known what love was until this point, but now I finally understood. It felt as though we were the only two people on the planet.

When you're in love, your body produces norepinephrine and adrenaline – basically that feeling that you're on a rollercoaster and might shit yourself. This can trigger physical responses, such as sweaty palms, racing heart, flushed cheeks and feelings of anxiety.

Here is an image of what love feels like:

Roses are red,
violets are blue,
I'm about to get my heart broken
and the culprit
is you.

OMG, I just thought of another.

Roses are red,
violets are blue,
in the snow
I did a poo.

Things were going good with July. In fact, better than good. They were going amazing. We were spending every weekend together, kissing, laughing, cuddling, like some couples do. The only issue was, we *weren't* a couple. One thing we'd never discussed with one another was our individual sexualities. It didn't seem relevant; we were in love so, who cares? I think we both dreaded this conversation in case we said something the other person didn't want to hear. Also, if you don't explicitly talk about something, you can pretend it isn't real. Until one day, she told me that she was going to the park with this boy. For the sake of this book, I'm going to call him Toby. I was hesitant, but I assumed they were going just as friends. After all, she and I loved each other. The next day, she told me that Toby had asked her out, and she had said yes.

My heart absolutely broke in my chest. I didn't understand. Why had she got a boyfriend when she and I were practically dating? I was *so* hurt. And I was honest with her, and told her how hurt and confused I was. She then went on to tell me some of the following:

'We can't do this any more.'

'It was a mistake.'

'It shouldn't have happened.'

'I'm not gay.'

'I just want to be your friend.'

'It cannot happen again.'

My whole world had been pulled from underneath me. My happiness had been snatched. *Not* in the good *Drag Race* way. I moped around school for a long time. My friends didn't know what was up with me, and the worst thing was, I couldn't tell them, because it was a secret. Nobody knew. If my straight friends were heartbroken, they could show it, and everyone would support them and give them advice. I didn't get that, because I couldn't reveal the source of my heartbreak. I wasn't ready to out myself, and I was already conscious of July's feelings about us.

Trying to conceal the way I was feeling was so incredibly difficult. I was acting out more than usual, misbehaving more than usual, and losing all interest in pretty much everything. July and I were still talking in school, because we physically couldn't stay away from each other even if we tried, but we were distant and unhappy. She didn't talk about Toby around me. I didn't want to hear anything about him. It made my blood boil.

She eventually invited me round for a sleepover again. I was completely prepared for it to be different to every other sleepover we'd ever had, now that she had a boyfriend and had told me everything between us shouldn't have happened. I had tried to mentally prepare myself to just see her as a friend. Nothing more. We watched scary films and we listened to our favourite songs, like we always had done. Before, we had always held hands in bed, or played with each other's hands. She had the most beautiful hands. This time, our hands were stiff by our sides. We barely made eye contact. It breaks my heart when I think about it – we were trying to force ourselves to not do something we enjoyed based on what we thought was right and wrong. Fuck that.

We lay down, with the lights off, ready to go to sleep. It felt so wrong. So uncomfortable. I faced away from her. I remember just staring into the distance for a long time, trying not to cry. I didn't want her to know I was upset. Just as I'd managed to hold back my tears, I felt her arm come around me and gently turn me over. She held my face. Our noses were touching. Tears left our eyes, and then we kissed. Until the sun came up. Again and again.

The next day was the same routine; I got my Skittles and energy drink, and took the 11 bus home. I'd missed her and her touch and her company so much, I finally felt like myself again. It was a release. I dreaded checking my phone, because I imagined I'd receive a text saying she regretted it, even though she had instigated it. I was wrong, but what I did receive was even *worse*.

*

I've told you already that I've got a short attention span. For me, this is too many words in one go. It's heavy to write, so I imagine it could be heavy to read, especially if you can relate to it on a personal level. If I wasn't writing about myself, there's a risk I'd be overwhelmed by this point, and believe it or not, I have your best interests at heart. So, here's an *X Factor* Worst Auditions Crossword for you to enjoy before we continue. If you get them all right, we can absolutely be friends:

ACROSS:
2. I REALLY WANNA SLAP YOU NOW
3. SHE PUNCHED HER, IN THE FACE
5. SHE GOT THAT SUPER SEXY SWINGING THING
7. BETTER THAN MADONNA

DOWN:
1. I ASPIRE TO BE, ME
2. CAN I JUST CHECK THE WORDS
3. COME ON MOVE YOUR BODY
4. WHERE'S YOUR BRAIN IN YOUR MIDDLE TOE?
6. WHAT HAVE WE DONE TO THE WORLD?

July hadn't messaged me to see if I got home OK, which was unlike her. So, I messaged her and told her how much I'd missed her. She eventually replied, and the only thing she told me was that she was going out with Toby that day. My heart dropped. *Why would you kiss me again then tell me you're going out with your boyfriend? Surely you should dump him and just be with me? That's what you want, so why aren't you doing it?* None of it made sense to me at that time. She just carried on as normal, as if my feelings didn't at all matter or exist. I tried to convince myself I was worth more than that, and that I shouldn't put up with being treated that way. That resolution would last until I found myself in her bed again, only for the same routine to play out. Settling for feeling not good enough. This was the way it was for about a year. A whirlwind of not knowing where I stood, being told to go away one minute, and being pulled in the next. It was exhausting . . . but also thrilling. I was willing to feel the pain if it meant having somewhere to express myself and my feelings for July. I'd take hurt over nothing. It was the only thing I could feel.

So, you know what that means: time to wrap up 2009 before we continue. Join me in reminiscing.

Musical interlude no. 3: 2009

Here are my top ten songs from 2009:

'Knock You Down' –Keri Hilson feat. Kanye West and Ne-Yo
'Down' – Jay Sean feat. Lil Wayne
'Halo' – Beyoncé
'Circus' – Britney Spears
'Run This Town' – Jay-Z feat. Rihanna and Kanye West
'Whatcha Say' – Jason Derulo
'LoveGame' – Lady Gaga

'If I Were a Boy' – Beyoncé
'The Fear" – Lily Allen
'Battlefield' – Jordin Sparks

Other iconic 2009 throwbacks:

- multi-coloured tights
- Primark cardigans
- statement belts
- BlackBerry Messenger
- *Avatar*
- Obama
- *Hannah Montana: The Movie*
- Lady Gaga's MTV VMA performance

JULY (PART TWO)

Now we've cleared that up, back to my heartbreak. I found it impossible to stay away from July, even though I was hurting myself in the process. The conversations about 'us' were becoming more and more frequent, and I'd feel the same sense of regret in the morning every time I spent a night with July. I didn't regret being with her – I couldn't even if I wanted to. I regretted letting myself feel hurt over and over again. The nights were as perfect as ever, as if nothing else mattered. Our phones were on the floor on silent, so nobody could disturb this time together. Then the morning came, and it was time to get back to our lives. Her and Toby, looking happy to the outside world, and me and my sadness. I knew she didn't like him. Not the way she liked me. In my eyes, he didn't deserve her. He could never love her the way that I did. Nobody could.

Over time, the nights we were spending together stopped being full of love and intimacy, and I was becoming unhappy. All of the time. Was this the heartbreak feeling people talk about? I found myself listening to songs that reminded me of July all the time. 'Hate That I Love You' by Rihanna feat. Ne-Yo suddenly had a whole new meaning. I'd go out of my way in school to find her. I wouldn't say anything; I just wanted her to see me. I figured if she'd see me, it might remind her of what we had together – or what we'd had. If she took a long time to reply to me, it would ruin my day. If I saw her walk into the canteen, I'd make sure I laughed the loudest, so she knew I was doing fine. Even though I obviously wasn't. I was completely self-destructing over her. Until I decided to give her a taste of her own medicine. I got myself a boyfriend, who, believe it or not, was *also* called Toby. What are the chances? Poor Tobys – both dating girls who were dating each other and had no real interest in them whatsoever. Bless.

I got the reaction I wanted from July. She was jealous. I'd make sure to upload photos of me and Toby, and when we were all out together, I'd make a point of kissing him in front of her. Seeing her face drop or hearing her tell me she didn't like seeing us together gave me the greatest pleasure. Is that a mean thing to say? It wasn't because I liked seeing her in pain; I would never have wished that upon her. It was because her being bothered told me that she cared, and that she *did* love me. Her actions were saying what her words no longer did.

I know, of course, that in the long term, this method wasn't healthy, but it was giving me the hit I needed at the time. The kissing with July was becoming less frequent, and when it did happen, she'd always say afterwards, 'That's the last time, OK?' Once I remember us kissing and her saying it was the last time, and then she kissed me again five minutes later and said, 'No, *that* was the last time.' It's kind of funny, until I remember that we were forcing ourselves to stop doing what we enjoyed together – and for what? Because of what other people would say or think? Sometimes we'd sit next to each other in the canteen and our hands would touch under the table. Then somebody would come over, and we'd quickly let go and avoid eye contact with one another. It felt like forbidden love. So I'm sure you can guess what this one is called . . .

Forbidden Love

I've loved you since the moment I saw you,
that's the only thing there is;
my lips will spare your ears the words,
and you'll feel it in my kiss.
When I press myself against you,
I know that you'll know,
that my heart is gripping tightly,
to a feeling I'll never let go.
And when I explore your shoulder
with my pretty poet's tongue,
you'll feel me writing lyrics,
of a song I'll leave unsung.
But those words are just words,
that mean as much in my head,
so I'll kiss you in the silence,
where I'll keep my words instead.
You pretend not to notice,
because that's the safest thing to do,
but I promise I'll stay by your side
and never tell you, that I love you.

NIAMH

During this confusing on-and-off-again phase with July, my behaviour
and my mental state had deteriorated so much that Miss Mooney had
started to notice. She called me into her coffee-stinking office for a chat.
Just the coffee *smell* made me wide-eyed, so god knows how she felt. She
told me she'd arranged for me to talk to a counsellor called Niamh. Until
this point, I'd always thought counsellors were people whom adults spoke
to about their marriage issues. That's what I'd seen in films, anyway. Plus,
I didn't want my mum to know I was talking to some counsellor at school,

because then she'd ask me what was wrong, and I wasn't ready to tell her about my love life, or lack of. I told Miss Mooney I didn't want to and that I'd be fine without it – until she told me that the sessions would take place during lesson times, and my mum didn't have to know. She'd won me over.

I remember my first session with my counsellor, Niamh. She was Irish and had a kind but stern voice. I liked her instantly. She made me feel safe and heard for the first time in my life. I felt myself relaxing around her, and telling her things that I didn't know I needed to. We'd sit in this tiny room behind the school called the Tac Room, facing each other. It was usually freezing in there and smelled of playdough. Niamh would look so intently at me when I spoke, making brief notes in between, which I always tried to read but couldn't. She asked me a lot of questions, which I liked because I obviously loved talking about myself. We spoke about everything, from school to homelife, from aspirations to how much I liked to drink at the weekend. She was never judgemental about what I did, or how I spent my time. She listened so deeply to all of my views, worries and opinions, and I never felt unseen by her. So much so that she is *still* my therapist today. It's been eleven years, and she now knows me better than I know myself. I can confidently say she has helped me in ways for which I could never repay her.

Here are her notes from our earliest sessions:

June 2011
Issues with boyfriend (no names). Seeing someone but not in a relationship – he sees her when he wants to. Uses her then says they can't go on like this, which makes her feel bad and used – she gets v upset and jealous when she sees him talking or mixing with girls.

She loves him and says she can never imagine herself being with anyone else – feels obsessed.
Rollercoaster – not in control

Going to try and be strong and allow him to make contact
with her. They have had loads of arguments and he has
certain rules for her but not for him. If she can not make contact
today, it will tell him that she is taking back some control.

17/6/11
Wrote out the good and bad things about "Lad?".
Still won't tell name – she is totally obsessed by "him" and
her whole life revolves round "him" – she is 80% unhappy
as he treats her bad and wrote out how she feels.
Going to think of ways of putting small changes into place
– she needs to change self and not others.

1/7/11
Very low – still not giving out any info on who it may be
– spoke to Jane as I was v concerned about her emotional
state – could it be female???

8/7/11
A little happier today – "he" has admitted that "he" likes
someone else.

13/7/11
More accepting "he" is seeing someone.
But she still sees "him" when he asks. Going on holiday to
Benidorm and is worried that he will not want to see her when
she is back and write things on Facebook to annoy her
– she needs to rise above it and put more of a value on herself
as he will prob do it to ruin her holiday
– before she was a very high 10 in how she dealt with him – now
she is a 6/7 so it's reducing – more belief in self!

Notice how the word 'he' is in quotation marks? Niamh knew from the second I opened my mouth that I wasn't really talking about a boy. She must have a great gaydar. Iconic, really.

I started seeing Niamh once a week. I was finally getting the advice I so desperately needed, and I was sharing things for the very first time. The relief I felt was immense. Like a weight lifted from my shoulders. I was still hurting, but I felt a little lighter now, knowing that I could talk about my true feelings. I eventually told Niamh that the 'he' was July; she told me she knew. She had just been waiting for me to feel comfortable enough to tell her.

I felt like all I did was cry during those hours with Niamh. I cried and cried and cried. I cried so much that my eyes started to sting. I guess I was letting out years of pent-up emotions. One session was so bad that I told Niamh I wanted to go to sleep and never wake up again. I'll never forget that day. It was the day before the school holidays, which meant a whole six weeks of being at home, and July and I weren't talking at the time. I know kids my age were mad for the school holidays; they couldn't wait. I was the complete opposite. The longer I was in school, the better I felt. I'd keep things together for the most part in school; it was when I got home, when I had nothing to distract me, that I'd drown in my own feelings. At that time, Niamh was only available to me during school hours. When I found myself at home, I'd google things like 'how to get over someone' and 'how to stop loving someone', and if that didn't work, I'd bash my head on my own wall to give myself something new to cry about. Wish that was a joke. #LiveLaughLove.

Here's a list of what I'd usually find in answer to my Google searches, followed by my own internal responses:

> Write down all the reasons you love this person. Now think about whether you're receiving the same commitment from them.
> *Obviously I'm not, why would you say that?*

Remind yourself of the reasons why it isn't working.
That's all I ever fuckin' do.

Distract yourself with other activities.
Simply don't want to.

Be honest with them.
No.

Avoid constantly checking in on them.
Impossible.

Plan your future without them in it.
It doesn't exist.

Take time to focus on yourself
Who? Lol.

JULY (PART THREE)

When I wasn't getting life-changing advice from Google, I'd watch porn. It was the only thing I could do that provided temporary relief from my heartache. As soon as the porn finished, I, of course, felt 10,000 times worse. Seeing two fake, stiletto-wearing, long-nailed straight women clumsily attempting to scissor each other while being filmed by a misogynistic heterosexual man with his dick out ultimately gave me something *else* to cry about.

You should know that I *survived* the 2009 school holidays. They were the longest six weeks of my life. I had started drunk-crying, though. I'd only ever been on the receiving end of a drunk cry when my friends would sob over their horrible boyfriends as their supposedly waterproof mascara streamed down their faces. I remember feeling relieved that I wouldn't ever shed a tear over a boy, but instead I found myself sobbing over a girl that I was in love with, who was too ashamed to openly love me back. Sigh. Gem had guessed what was going on; after all, she's my best friend. She used to try and give me advice that I never followed.

Oh, by the way, Toby eventually caught wind that I wasn't really into him, and he dumped me. What a relief. I remember him knocking on for me once and my mum came into my room, like, 'Lovely Toby is at the door,' and I said, 'I'm going to see July, tell him I'm not home.' Mum *must* have known. July and her Toby broke up as well. Yes, I was happy about it.

You might be thinking of that one person who makes you feel that way. The person who makes you lose yourself. The person who hurts you continuously, but you just can't stay away from. Maybe you were also in the closet and know *exactly* what I'm talking about. Either way, I hope that you talk to your friends about this and get some good advice that you'll never follow.

I know counselling doesn't work for everyone, or that access to it isn't always available, but for me, it was the best thing I could do. What made it so difficult to try and manage these feelings before Niamh was that there wasn't anyone I felt like I could talk to about it, because then not only would I be outing myself, I'd also be outing July. It wasn't my place to do that.

Experiencing feelings of heartbreak for the first time is painful enough on its own; when you combine that with suppressing your sexuality, it's even worse. I was starting to hate myself, and my feelings. I don't blame July now. I did at the time, because I selfishly wasn't considering her own insecurities, just mine. July was suppressing her sexuality too, and in doing so was hurting me and causing me to suppress mine even more. Eventually, that led to us both being ashamed of being in love with one another. It breaks my heart.

I still wonder to this day if things might have been different, had we not been made to believe our feelings for each other were wrong. I was certain she was my person. The absolute love of my life. Maybe if things were different, I wouldn't be writing this book.

Have I mentioned that I'm writing a book?

*

OK, here's some more iconic reality TV to indulge in before we all start crying. This one is called 'Nothing of the Sort', by Tiffany Pollard. Take it away, Tiff:

Pretty much, I would let Gemma know
that she is a fat c*nt
and, um, the shoes that she gave me were
not something that I would particularly
buy for myself.

They were old-maiden type of shoes, and
she said that those shoes were meant to
be worn on a beautiful woman.

So if that is the case, she should have put
them back on the rack and she should have
never even purchased them, because she
was UNQUALIFIED to own those shoes if
that's the case.

And, um, I think that Gemma is just a
disgrace. She's a disgrace to women who are
actually beautiful and classy and, um, she
just doesn't have the vernacular she
thinks she possesses.

Somebody lied to her several times and
told her that she was fly, hot and sexy
and beautiful, and she's nothing like that.
She's nothing of the sort.

*

Time flies when you hate yourself and you're heartbroken, right? I don't even know what year we're in. Oh yeah, we're now at the end of 2010. I'm sure you're thinking, *More must have happened in the last two years than you just crying and watching porn?*

Nope.

Nothing more than that. I didn't notice much, anyway. I was so sad all the time, and everything just blurred into one. I was numb during my last two years of high school. I was still causing scenes and making people laugh, but I had a sadness inside of me that hadn't been there before. I switched it off in school, unless I saw July in the canteen. On those occasions, I'd go to the toilets for five minutes to cry before composing myself to be the class clown once more. There were now a lot of sad songs occupying my iPod Shuffle. I would listen to Rihanna's 'California King Bed' on repeat; July and I had loved that song. 'Fight for This Love' had faded into the background; I didn't feel happy when I listened to it any more. I didn't feel happy as a result of most things any more. July and I had locked our love away. We tried to be just friends, and it never worked; I believe it's impossible to be just friends when you're in love with each other. We carried on loving each other from afar. That was the easiest way. Even though we were both in agony.

Anyway, let's wrap up all of this heartbreak and love stuff, because, quite frankly, it's depressing me. Is it depressing you? If I'm honest, I could go on about this for the rest of the book; it's been over eleven years and the pain still hasn't left me. Apparently, you never get over your first love. Which I find incredibly fucking annoying. It's a life-changing experience. For me, it was also a life-changing lesson, that took me years of work to learn: *never* be ashamed of who you truly are. You can only hide yourself for so long, and it's damaging. Be at peace with who you are, and others will be at peace with you. Wow, am I life guru?

Musical interlude no. 4: 2010

I hope you didn't think I'd forget to wrap up 2010, one of *the* most iconic years for music and pop culture. It's a year I always go back to when I want to feel real nostalgia.

Here are my top songs from 2010:

'Love the Way You Lie' – Eminem feat. Rihanna
'Bad Romance' – Lady Gaga
'Dynamite' – Taio Cruz
'Nothin' on You' – B.o.B feat. Bruno Mars
'BedRock' – Young Money
'Find Your Love' – Drake
'Club Can't Handle Me' – Flo Rida feat. David Guetta
'Only Girl (In the World)' – Rihanna
'Un-Thinkable' – Alicia Keys
'Replay' – Iyaz
'Te Amo' – Rihanna
'Seek Bromance' – Avicii
'What's My Name?' – Rihanna feat. Drake
'Man Down' – Rihanna

Other iconic things from 2010:

- *127 Hours*
- leggings becoming a thing
- the cinnamon challenge
- Drake's *Thank Me Later* album
- Matt Cardle winning *The X Factor*
- the lesbian scene in *Black Swan*

- Jesus bracelets
- DIY tie-dye
- Lady Gaga's meat dress
- Blanche dying in *Corrie* (RIP)
- Rihanna releasing one of the *best* albums in the world, *Loud*
- Nicki Minaj's *Pink Friday* album

HARRY POTTER

It was also the year that *Harry Potter and the Deathly Hallows: Part 1* was released. You might remember from my poem about Luke that he and I loved Harry Potter. I remember being in bed with him and watching this film for the first time. We were eating Morrisons sausage rolls and Monster Munch, and sharing a big bottle of 7Up. He had loads of cool wands that he'd got from America; one of them was Lucius Malfoy's, a tall, snake-headed spear. I always thought it was so cool. So did he. He promised to give me one of the wands one day. They're currently in the second drawer down in his bedroom; I look at them when I go in there sometimes. Stacey says that when I have my own place one day, I can have them and keep them in a special cabinet. I can't wait for that day.

I remember when the film finished, we were literally screaming in bed, because we couldn't bear to wait for *Part 2* to be released. I think we must have watched *Part 1* more than fifteen times while we waited for *Part 2*. I love watching it now. It'll always remind me of him.

IT'S NOT A PHASE, MOM

OK, so we're somehow in 2011. Where has the time gone? If I'm honest, I barely remember this year. I was hurting and couldn't bear to be leaving school yet. I just tried to keep myself busy, by simply being myself. That was exhausting enough. I got back to snogging boys to pass the time. I would just close my eyes and picture July to get me through it.

I had good friends around me at this time, though. Danny knew I was sad, and his way of cheering me up would be to say, 'Stop fucking crying about it, you miserable cow.' Surprisingly, this worked – at least, sometimes. Other times, we'd dip tampons into the watery red sauce that is Pasta King and throw them around the canteen to spook the dinner ladies; that also cheered me up.

Now that I didn't have July as often as usual, I needed a new obsession. I still loved Cheryl, but I needed something more. I'm an obsessive person, and I constantly need to find new ways to keep my mind occupied. And so, 2011 became the year that I got really into dubstep and drum and bass.

Typing that sentence just gave me the ick.

I was about to go through a personality crisis – AGAIN. My shit hair had started to grow out and now looked even worse, so I decided to shave the side of it and dye it a dark purple, because that obviously screams: 'I am mentally stable – and straight.' I bought myself a pair of creepers that gave me the biggest blisters known to womankind, along with a tie-dye denim jacket with massive spikes all over, and leggings with upside-down crosses. The jacket smelled of old people, and you could see every crevice of my arse in the leggings. Can you *believe* it? Who was I trying to be? Danny was going through the same phase, so we'd try and rock it together – unsuccessfully. We became obsessed with Skrillex and went to his concerts, which basically involved being absolutely leathered by a bunch of sweaty moshers. It wasn't my scene, but I needed something. We'd go there to purposefully get into fights. It was a nice way to release anxiety and anger at the time. I wouldn't recommend it now, though . . .

I'd also got really into Tumblr, and creating a mysterious, dark aesthetic on there became my personality for a while. My bio was 'DROP THE BASS'. I'll give you a second to recover from that. I used to repost pictures of men with tattoos drinking a bottle of Jack Daniels, smoking a spliff and sitting on the edge of a very tall building, looking like they'd gone three years without a shower. How arty and original.

Isn't it interesting that, as kids, we tend to go through multiple phases? I guess we're trying to figure out what social bracket we belong in. If you were born around 1996, here's a list of general phases you might have gone through as a teen:

The Artsy Phase – You channel all of your angst into shit paintings that your mum shares on Facebook, or you post poems on Myspace as part of your indie 'blog'.

The Vegetarian Phase – You watch *Charlotte's Web* and decide bacon is no longer for you. Eating nothing but veg is trendy.

The 'I Hate My life' Phase – Woe is you. Everything is shit, and your mum asking you if you're OK is enough to make you blow your lid. You repost pictures on Tumblr that say: 'Just hold me while I crumble in your arms'.

The Emo/Goth/Scene Phase – Hayley Williams becomes your new crush, and you like it when your trainers get dirty. You wear bracelets that say 'WTF' and 'OMG' and you enjoy saying 'RAWR xd'.

The Shaving your Monobrow Phase – You go straight down the middle with your mum's Bic razor she uses to shave her fanny. Your eyebrows look like they've had an argument. People at school laugh.

The *Twilight* Phase – You go around thinking you're a translucent, sparkly vampire, while also trying to be as mysterious as Bella, and saying things like: 'And so the lion fell in love with the lamb.'

The Lying Phase – OK . . . this isn't a phase. It's my personality.

I'm sure there are many more phases; these are just the ones I'm familiar with. I guess it's because we're trying to 'find' ourselves? I feel like, as humans, we spend most of our lives trying to 'find' ourselves. *Where* are we? Do we ever *really* find ourselves? I've never understood that phrase, but all I knew at this point was that this personality crisis was confusing the fuck out of me. My mum would say things to me like, 'That's an interesting jumper,' which translated to, 'What the fuck is that jumper all about, ya weirdo?'

I was the only one out of me, Stacey and Matthew to go through a 'weird' stage – as in, experimenting with different and questionable styles. Stacey and Matthew only ever gave nineties chav: Ellesse jumpers, Kappa buttoned trousers and Nike TNs. All hand-me-downs, of course. Matthew told me that when Stacey would see him in school and she was with her friends, she'd say stuff like, 'Err, get my jumper off now, you tramp.' That made me laugh, 'cause if he was a tramp, she was one too, and they shared the same clothes. They also moved out and had kids at the same age I was still sleeping in bed with my mum sometimes, so . . . They had to grow up quicker than I did, in some ways.

When July and I did talk, I'd send her all the new songs I was into at the time. She liked them. Sometimes we'd listen to them together. Sometimes, we'd kiss to them. Not as often, now.

As everything eventually does, my new obsession started to die down, and my sadness took over again. This need for a constant focus was draining me, mentally and physically. It felt as if I was never fulfilled, like I could never get enough of something. Even if I found myself feeling happy or at peace with a certain situation, I'd be quick to remind myself that things were still shit.

I remember once at the end of a school day, I saw July at the gates, and she completely ignored me. I walked home in the pissing-down rain and went and sat in a car park on the ground, crying my eyes out for hours before going home. It was like crying in the shower; I couldn't tell the difference between my tears and the rain any more. It all became one. I sat on the ground and wept until I had no tears left to cry. It wasn't just because July had ignored me. It was everything: not feeling good enough and never feeling fulfilled. I remember thinking that I wouldn't care if I got hit by a car on my way home; in fact, I kind of hoped that I would. I feel sad to admit that, because little did I know that the pain I was feeling now wouldn't even compare to pain I'd feel in the future. But at that time, at the age of fifteen, it felt like this would be my life forever. A constant state of unhappiness and shame about who I was.

I eventually got home, piss-wet through, and I got straight into bed. I remember there was no gas or electric, so I was freezing. I could see my breath in the air. I kept my shoes and coat on. I fell asleep in my soaking uniform and then went to school the next day without changing. Still damp and sad from the night before.

DRAMA (THE GOOD KIND)

Seeing Niamh was helping. I don't know where I would have been without her; I know I'd have been a lot worse than I was. One of the bits of advice she gave me was: 'Focus on what makes you happy.'

There was very little within school that made me happy at the time – but one thing I absolutely loved, which *won't* surprise you, was Drama.

I think it was during year nine we were allowed to pick our 'options', which basically meant picking the subjects we wanted to focus on in year ten. We were supposed to choose the ones that might help us get a university place or lead us down a particular career path. Drama was the only one I *wanted* to pick, but I *had* to pick three. So, I chose Drama, Health and Social Care and Religious Education. I'm sure you're thinking, *Why the fuck did you chose those?* Honestly, I don't know. I think I chose Health and Social Care because we got to play with a pretend baby, and I chose Religious Education to find out if God hates the gays. I actually ended up enjoying RE – I liked learning about different religions and their beliefs, even if those beliefs were that I deserved to be stoned and thrown off a tall building. #LiveLaughLove. I remember RE lessons often got super-heated; we'd debate subjects such as abortion and euthanasia, and I did actually learn a lot. Health and Social Care was a fun class. All of my mates were in it, and we had such a safe teacher; she was a right laugh. Even if she did used to send me out for saying the word 'tits' too much.

Drama was always different, though. It was the one lesson where I felt at home. I wanted my whole school day to just be Drama. I should probably tell you I wasn't one of those kids who had wanted to be an actor since birth. I didn't even know what 'being an actor' meant. All I knew was that I loved attention, I loved making up stories, and I loved making people laugh. When I'd watch films and TV as a kid, I assumed the people on the telly were just *there* – I didn't think about how they got there. I probably thought they were rich and just given that opportunity. (As I've entered the industry and got older, I've learned that I actually wasn't far off the mark with that theory.) I never thought the person on the screen could be me one day.

When I got a bit older, though, I told my mum that I wanted to try and 'do stuff' on the telly. It was too expensive to enrol me into local drama classes, and we just didn't have the money. She found a voucher in the paper for a stage school called Stagecoach; the voucher was an offer for a cheaper course. Even with the discount, it was expensive, but somehow Mum made it work. I was so excited, because I'd heard of Stagecoach before. Tracy Beaker (aka Dani Harmer) went there. I read that in *Mizz* magazine. Stagecoach had a great reputation for singing, acting and dancing classes. Before my first day, I'd been told to purchase their uniform: a black leotard, dancing shoes, black tights and a Stagecoach T-shirt. We'd just been able to afford the class with the discount, so buying the entire uniform was a no-go. I was embarrassed to be turning up without the clothes, but Mum assured me there would be plenty of other kids without them as well. I remember her saying, 'They can't expect everyone to be able to afford that.' I took her word for it, because after all, I was grateful that I was going. I turned up in a pair of old black leggings that had a hole in the crotch, one of Mum's black vest tops that smelled of cigs, and some hand-me-down trainers from Gemma. I got out of the car and Mum told me to smash it! I smiled and waved her off.

As I walked inside with a sandwich bag of coins, notes and a scrunched-up cut-out from the paper, I saw so many kids of all different ages rehearsing in the corridors. It was like *High School Musical*; that was the closest comparison I had in my head. I felt so out of place the second

I walked in there. Everyone looked like they were best friends already, and they *all* had the crisp, clean uniform on. Cheers, Mum. After the embarrassing handover of my sandwich bag of funds, I headed to my first lesson, which was a dance class. Let me just tell you, I am good at a lot of things; great, in fact. One thing I cannot do to save my life, though, is follow a dance routine. I have two left feet, and I don't have the attention span to learn a series of moves. I'm decent at freestyling after a couple of glasses of wine, but put me in a room and try and teach me a routine, and you will get *nowhere*. I have rhythm in the sheets and not in the streets. You're welcome. I soon discovered this. We were in this massive room full of mirrors, so not a single error of mine could be missed. By anyone.

Nobody said hello to me, or even welcomed me to the school, which upset me. I had planned what my first day would be like in my head: I'd go in there and the teacher would introduce me to the rest of the class, and everyone would want to be my friend instantly. I'd excel in every aspect of the school, and within a few weeks be given a huge, life-changing role on TV. The reality was nothing of the sort. I felt exposed in my vest top and leggings, and people were giving me dirty looks from every corner of the room, as if I didn't belong there. We started learning a routine to 'You Can't Stop the Beat' from *Hairspray*, and I simply couldn't keep up. I tried my fucking hardest, though. I wanted to prove to all of the posh kids with their judging looks and their new uniforms that I deserved to be there just as much as they did. I stood out like a sore thumb; everyone else was following the routine to a T. I was sweating, out of breath and simply embarrassed to be there. At the end of the class, the teacher came over to me and asked who I was. *Oh, now you want to know me?* I thought. She told me to practise the routine at home ready for the next class. *Great advice. Thanks.*

I tried to stick it out. I didn't want to disappoint my mum – I know she'd worked hard to get me there – but after a few months of failing at dance routines and having no friends, I gave it up. Every day there was damaging me more and more. It was just rubbing my face in what I didn't have, and it was making me uncomfortable and upset. Seeing the kids there every day getting picked up in their dad's newest BMW with their Stagecoach-branded water bottles and their shiny shoes. I bet they had parents and John Lewis PJs with fluffy carpets – and a PORCH! They *all* had porches in their gaffs. Let me tell you.

Rather than helping me succeed, it was just tarnishing the one thing I enjoyed. It was a harsh introduction to the impostor syndrome I still feel in such situations to this day. GCSE Drama was much more fun – and, most importantly, it was free.

Lesson learned: just because Tracy Beaker went there, doesn't mean it's any good.

When I think about it now, GCSE Drama was so funny. The small dramatic freeze-frames we'd create were BAFTA-worthy performance gold. You know the ones, where a kid would stand in the middle and we'd circle them, whispering, 'Smoking, drinking, sex,' and we'd repeat it until we started screaming it, and then the kid in the middle would drop to the floor, overwhelmed by the peer pressure, and then the lights would go off, and BANG! That's Drama, baby! Obviously one of the main reasons I loved it was because it involved very little written work (she says, while writing an entire *book*).

NEW DRINKING GAME: Drink every time I mention that I'm writing a book. Unless you're under eighteen, in which case, carry on reading and ignore this. Soz.

*

Musical interlude no. 5: 2011

2011's most iconic songs:

'E.T.' – Katy Perry feat. Kanye West
'Super Bass' – Nicki Minaj
'Just Can't Get Enough' – The Black Eyed Peas
'Look At Me Now' – Chris Brown feat. Lil Wayne and Busta Rhymes
'Sure Thing'– Miguel
'Price Tag' – Jessie J feat. B.o.B
'Coming Home' – Diddy–Dirty Money feat. Skylar Grey
'Yeah 3x' – Chris Brown
'Moment 4 Life' – Nicki Minaj feat. Drake
'Motivation' – Kelly Rowland feat. Lil Wayne
'We Found Love' – Rihanna feat. Calvin Harris

Other iconic things from 2011:

- Adele getting six Grammy nominations
- *Bridesmaids* (world's best film)
- *Harry Potter* finishing
- Beyoncé's baby announcement
- Kim K's seventy-three-day marriage
- planking
- Little Mix being the first girl band to win *The X Factor*
- the Sophie-and-Sian lesbian storyline in *Corrie*
- me getting a tattoo

I remember telling my Drama teacher at the time that I wanted to be an actor and that's all I wanted to do. She was encouraging, but told me how hard it was, and said that I should have a backup plan. Little did I know this would be the first of *hundreds* of times I'd be told this.

Spoiler: I didn't make a backup plan. In my head, that's all I wanted to do, and I *would* do it. No matter what it took. Was this about to become my new obsession? Yes, yes it was. I finally had something I wanted to do, something I knew I was good at. Most importantly, it didn't involve changing my hair again. I didn't know at this stage what *kind* of actor I wanted to be, I just knew that I was good at entertaining people and enjoyed attention.

I would often talk to Niamh about my future and what I wanted. She was always very encouraging; she still is. Here are her notes from one of our 2011 sessions:

> 10 years from now – Sophie G
> Acting job on the TV. Something within performing arts. Happily married, with a car and a house. Can afford lots of holidays.

Can we just acknowledge the fact that I thought I'd be married by the age of twenty-five, with a car and a house? I'm twenty-five right now, and I'm not married, I can't drive, I don't have a house, and I can't afford lots of holidays. However, I *am* an actor, and I have been on TV! Fuck marriage and a house, right? I achieved my dream!

Hold your horses, you'll see why this is particularly special later on. I don't want to spoil the story.

While rehearsing for my GCSE Drama performance, I'd started looking into colleges with good acting courses. There were a few in my area, but I knew that all my peers were going to these colleges, and I decided that I needed a fresh start. I didn't want to be around anyone or anything that I associated with school, as inevitably that all led back to July, and my heart was too fragile over that situation. I wasn't strong enough to feel it any more. I knew that if I wanted to be a successful actor, I needed to put all of my time and energy into that goal, and I could only achieve that if I started afresh. I also liked the idea of going to a college where nobody knew me. I could just start again – and this time, ideally, not fall in love with someone who wasn't available to me.

So, I found a college in Salford called Pendleton, which specialised in performing arts. They had their own two-year acting course, which was drama-school accredited, and they also had an impressive alumni list, which I obviously wanted to be a part of. It was going to take me a walk and two buses to get there for a 9am start, which would have meant getting up at 6.30am every morning to travel into town, and then on to Salford. It was a big commitment for me, but one that I was seriously considering. Everyone around me was encouraging. Family, friends and Niamh all told me to go for it. My dad was worried at first – he didn't like the idea of me travelling that far every day – but I managed to talk him round. I always do.

Before I knew it, the end of my time at school was fast approaching. I was both excited for my next chapter and terrified at the thought of change. I think, as humans, we're hard-wired to resist change. The fear of the unknown and the uncertainty of new beginnings terrify us. Despite my longing for a fresh start, I've never coped well with change. I'm very particular in my ways, and anything that goes against routine stresses me out, so you can imagine my response to leaving behind everything I'd known for the last five years.

I went on the ol' Google and found this: metathesiophobia, the fear of change. Apparently, this particular phobia can lead to extreme anxiety, panic attacks and even suicidal thoughts.

Suicidal thoughts. So change can literally make you want to unalive yourself. Makes sense to me. For someone who doesn't like changes, I sure made a lot of them after I left school. Even though they scare us, changes can bring out the best in us.

LEAVERS' BOOK

I was ready for my change, but I needed to absorb as many memories from school as possible. So I got myself a leavers' book in which to store these memories. A leavers' book is basically a £2.50 lined Pukka Pad notebook from big Tesco that you hand around to people you don't really like so they can write you a goodbye message that you'll never read again. How ironic.

Just before I sat my GCSEs, my mum was supposed to be going to Portugal with her boyfriend at the time. They split up, so she invited me instead. I shouldn't have gone, really, because I needed to revise, but in true me-style, I went anyway. I remember spending most of the holiday thinking about July. I couldn't really enjoy myself, which was a shame. We didn't have much money to do stuff, so we'd just sit and play cards in the hotel reception.

Before I went away, I'd left my 'leavers' book' with a friend to get people to sign it. July and I weren't talking at the time. I'd kissed her boyfriend. On purpose. I didn't do it because I wanted to; I did it because I wanted to hurt her, and I wanted her attention, good or bad. She was more hurt that *I* had kissed *him*, than that he had kissed me . . . if that makes sense. Anyway, my friend still managed to get July to write me a message in my book. It's the only message that I still reread sometimes. It's six pages long, and on the back of the last page is a photo of us both. She ended the message with: 'Don't wear your heart on your sleeve. x' – a piece of advice that, surprisingly enough, I *didn't* go on to follow.

When I got back from my little holiday, I did OK in my GCSEs, given the circumstances. I got a B in English and an A in Drama; that's all that mattered to me. I failed Maths and got Cs and Ds in everything else. And guess what? Nobody – and I mean nobody – has ever asked me for my GCSE results. This is solely my opinion, but despite the way our schools try to convince us that we'll amount to nothing if we don't smash our GCSEs, I just don't think that's true.

Fucking hell – I feel like we've unpacked so much during these school years. Maybe you've read this section and felt at home with shared experiences, or maybe you've read it and thought, *What the fuck is wrong with this girl?* and cannot relate to any of it. Either way, I think we've learned some valuable lessons. Let's revisit them:

1. Don't let the people around you influence the decisions you do or do not make. You are your own person and you deserve to be happy, whatever that looks like.
2. Don't drink until you end up in hospital, and don't tell the medical professionals you're better than them.
3. Don't let yourself believe you don't belong in certain places. You deserve to be there just as much as everyone else, regardless of your financial situation, dance ability and lack of uniform.
4. Don't feel ashamed for watching porn. Everyone does it, whether they admit to it or not.
5. Don't drink White Lightning; it tastes like petrol.
6. Don't be embarrassed for seeking help. Instead, be proud of your bravery in recognising that you need it.
7. Remember that feelings are usually temporary, and there is always light at the end of the tunnel – you just have to find it.
8. Don't poo in the snow and then write about it.

Just before finishing school, we were given an *official* leavers' book. It had awards in it that teachers and students voted on: things like 'Most likely to be a millionaire', or 'Best laugh'. I won the award titled 'Most likely to win *Big Brother*'. I can't even lie to you, I was chuffed. It takes some real personality to win a personality show, right? So if I was sure of anything, it was that I had a memorable personality. In other words, I was a gobshite.

OK, let's finish this section with some iconic messages from my leavers' book that I've just read for the first time in ten years. They were all written by my previous teachers, and they all have an interesting theme, which I feel is testament to my character . . . you can decide what that is.

To 'Soph'

I will miss you a lot. You have taught me new things (like YOLO) and that a fifteen-year-old can get a tattoo. I'm sure you will do very well at being a famous actress. Make sure you don't forget me when you are a big star. I hope when you leave, I see you in a year's time with crazy-coloured hair (I suggest blue).

Lots of love and good luck – Miss Houlden xxx

Sophie,

What has been the most enjoyable thing about teaching you has been seeing you progress. You have come so far from the place you were in in year ten to where you are now. You put so much effort into your exam. Thank you. Despite what you might think, it has been a pleasure teaching you – your folder is fab! Be confident, be happy and make the most of life. It's short and goes fast. Follow your dreams – even if they're too big to fit into your head. I genuinely wish you every success in the future. Thanks for being so bonkers.

Miss Pridding
Drama
x

Hey Sophie,

God! I can't believe you are a grown-up and leaving! That's kinda crazy – a bit like you were in year seven, eight and nine when you

were mine! I wish you all the best in whatever you choose to
do after this place.

>All the best little Sophie (Cheryl)
>Mr Warhurst, tutor from the PAST x

Sophie,

My relaxing memory of you:

Sophie: ARGH I'M GOING MENTAL !
Me: OK.

The more that annoyed you, the more it amazed me,
as you can probably tell! Best of luck in the future. I would love to say
it's been a pleasure, but you're pretty crazy!

>Mr McGuigan

Dear Sophie,

I will miss your enthusiasm to attend PE lessons, especially in year
eleven. You would make a great personal assistant. Best wishes for the
future. Keep dancing! (the hustle)

>Miss Pike

Dear Sophie,

I think we will always remember your singing. You have matured into a pleasant and friendly person. I wish you the best of luck. Keep active and enjoy life!

Miss W (Goose)

Dear Sophie,

We have a lot of memories in PE, you've been a pain in the backside. No kit, but as you've got older, you became a bit better. Don't forget when you win an award that I was your PE teacher and to mention me.

I will not miss the singing.

Mrs Hardicar

Dear Soph,

My, my, my. How you have changed, developed, matured! You have come such a long way Sophie, particularly in the past twelve months, and it is just credit to you for continuing to commit yourself to Kingsway. I do hope that you will look back at school with a smile, and know that through it all, school was a good place for you.
Don't change (maybe the odd tweak here and there). Be true to yourself. Be whoever you want to be. Most of all, be happy.
Take care, mad, smiley, lovely Sophie.

Miss Mooney

College

HOUSE PARTIES

During the 2012 summer holidays, just before college, I turned sixteen. It was finally legal to have sex. Woo-fucking-hoo. My mum let me have a big party at our gaff; I absolutely loved it. I'd always been to everyone else's houses for parties up until this moment, and I never thought I'd host my own.

Don't you think house parties back in the day went absolutely *off*? I used to go to proper posh houses for parties in Bramhall. I had a lot of mates that lived in that area, and I used to chill round there at the weekends. I remember one party I went to; the guy had a massive heated swimming pool in his back garden. You can only *imagine* the chaos. I was drunk, swimming with my friends, with this guy's boxers on and my push-up Primark bra that was obviously too big. Mascara all over my face, screaming the lyrics to 'The Motto' by Drake, with a bottle of Glen's vodka in my hand. Those were the days. Behind the swimming pool was a really cute little outhouse with fairy lights, and his kitchen was all open-plan. It was the perfect location for a party, and people spoke about it for weeks after. I also went to house parties without swimming pools. Proper little houses with barely any room to move, but we had just as much of a good time. I think it's not about where you are, it's about who you're with. Also, there was always so much going on. I used to love the house-party gossip the morning after.

Here's a list of my favourite things about house parties:

- You don't have to queue up outside to get in somewhere or to go for a wee (not as much, anyway).
- You don't have to pay extortionate money for drinks.
- You can choose the music that's played.
- There is room to dance.
- There is a kitchen, so you can make toast.
- Bonus points if they have pets you can stroke.

I never thought I'd be able to have my own party, though, because I was always too embarrassed to have my mates round to my house when I was in school. In hindsight, there was nothing wrong with my house. It just needed a bit of decorating and a deep clean. Most of my friends had gorgeous houses; or at least, they looked gorgeous to me. They had colour schemes in their kitchens and cushions on their sofas. They also had handwash dispensers in their bathrooms. Even that was a bit posh. We had a bar of Imperial Leather soap with the little red sticker on it, and it was so worn down it was just permanently stuck to the side of the sink. We also never had any carpet on the stairs, so if one of my mates came round, I'd always say, 'Oh we're just in the middle of decorating, mind the nails.' 'Decorating' that lasted more than ten years . . . Once I had one of my friends from Bramhall to stay, and my mum spent all day cleaning the house – she'd even painted the living room and washed the curtains because she didn't want me to feel embarrassed. Then I did that typical thing of saying, 'Oh, I'm so sorry about the mess; we're just in the middle of doing the house up,' while my mum sat on the sofa, exhausted after scrubbing the gaff from top to bottom. I'm annoyed at myself now for feeling like I had to do that. Where I lived shouldn't have concerned my friends. It never actually did, mind – it was just my own insecurities and worries that took over. I think that's why I'm so obsessed with making my space so cosy and comfortable now, because I hardly had that as a kid. These days, I could honestly spend an entire day in Ikea, choosing everything I'd buy if I was rich. Like a massive fluffy rug.

Anyway, we decided to have my sixteenth mostly in the garden. We had a really long garden, so it was ideal. Somebody came round to cut the grass and the bushes and get everything ready, and when it was done it looked so nice. Mum hired a cheap gazebo and some massive speakers. We absolutely raided Quality Save for all their shite cheap booze, and I bought a dress from River Island that I kept the tag in so I could take it back the next day. I was so pleased with it all, and felt really proud to have my mates round – and I know that meant a lot to my mum, too. She'd had the downstairs bathroom done especially, and painted the kitchen with an old pot of paint we'd found in the shed. For once, I wasn't worried about what people were thinking of me or my house; I was feeling proud. Not only was this my sixteenth birthday party, I also viewed it as a goodbye party to school. A goodbye to that routine and those friends. I know that sounds brutal, but it's true.

I didn't know it at the time, but it really was a farewell party. We'd spent five years together, but that was the last time I saw a lot of those people. I was ready for a new journey and a fresh start. I also kissed three boys that night, all in different spots in the garden. They were all fit. I did it in front of July, obviously. She stayed over, but didn't kiss me in bed that night. I was sad about it.

I remember picking Luke up outside, and everyone told me how cute and cheeky he was. There's a picture of him holding an unopened bottle of beer, pretending to drink it. He is now my favourite memory of that night.

NEW BEGINNINGS

After the fiascos of my final years in school, you might be thrilled to know that I got into college. I had to audition. It was my first-ever audition, and I was absolutely petrified. I did a monologue from a play called *Two*, which was the same thing chosen by almost everyone else auditioning. I, of course, didn't know this until I got there and realised seven-tenths of the room were doing the same speech as me. I remember walking into the room, and there were three members of staff sitting behind a table, smiling at me, with notebooks and pens. It was like *The X Factor*. There was even a little mark on the floor for me to stand on.

('Can you stand on the X, please, Ariel . . . is there a problem with that?'

'No, no problem. But can I get on with singing now?')

My legs were literally shaking, and when I opened my mouth to say hello, no words came out. You know that feeling when you just freeze, and there's absolutely nothing you can do about it? My throat felt like I'd swallowed a mouthful of sand. It was one of those moments. They could obviously see how nervous I was, and they told me to relax and have fun. I couldn't have been *less* relaxed, and I was far from having fun; I thought I was going to physically shit myself. Again.

I somehow managed to get through it – I so wish I could watch it back now, because I bet it was awful, and so funny. I didn't know how to act then. All I taught myself was to remember the words. I didn't know anything about feeling, recalling or being present. All that was in my head was getting the words from my brain to my mouth. They must have seen something in me, though, because I got in – either that, or they felt awfully sorry for me and knew I needed teaching. Either way, I was *so* excited. So excited at the thought of being someone and achieving something. It was going to become my newest focus, my biggest dream.

As I mentioned, the journey to my new college was long, and our gorgeous, kind government gave me a whole £15 a week towards my travel. This just about paid for my bus pass – and I no longer received a dinner token. Live, laugh, love!

On reflection, I don't think school preps you for college as well as they could. It's the little things that add up and stress you out. Even the thought of having to wear my own clothes everyday was overwhelming, let alone calling teachers by their first names, or being referred to as a 'young adult' – EW. I don't even feel like an adult at this very moment, so I certainly didn't when I was sixteen. It's a significant jump from school to college, and in a way, I was grieving school when I first left. I know some of you might be reading that thinking, *That's really sad, Soph – school was shite* – and I get it, I do, but to go from spending five years of your life with the same people, in the same place, following the same routine, for that to all just stop is a difficult adjustment. At least, it was for me. I also had so much built-up anxiety from school that didn't shift straight away. Ultimately, though, I was the one who had made the decision to go to a college where I knew absolutely nobody, miles away from my house. This just further demonstrates my abilities to be very impulsive and make huge decisions on a whim.

I have a prominent memory from my first year of college. I think it was November 2012, and we were lying on the floor doing breathing exercises (shout-out to the actors reading this; you know the one). We were instructed to just *feel* every part of ourselves on the floor. It goes a little something like this . . .

As you lie there, hearing these words, you can become aware of your breathing . . . in and out . . . that's right . . . you can notice how your body moves as you breathe in and out . . . and now you can place your attention on your head, your lovely head, and just start to slowly relax the muscles of the top of your head . . . and as you feel the relaxation spreading down to your forehead, you can allow the muscles of your forehead to simply relax . . . gently letting go of any tension . . . and as you do so, you can begin to notice how your ears can just relax and go quiet . . . and the little muscles around your eyes begin to let go and relax . . .

At this point, I was thinking *What in the artsy-fartsy is this*? My feet were twitching, and I was looking around the room, wondering when it was going to be over.

... slowly spreading gentle relaxation into your cheeks and jaw, as you simply relax the muscles of your jaw, dropping it gently as you continue to breathe in and out ... that's right ... and as your jaw muscles slowly let go, your tongue can begin to just hang loose, as you breathe in and out ... and then the relaxation spreads through your neck, noticing any areas of tension, slowly noticing the muscles of your neck relax and loosen up as you feel the tension dropping and your shoulders just relax ... that's right ...

I noticed the rest of the class was paying attention to the meditation, which meant nobody was paying *me* any attention. So I thought I'd give it a good go. I closed my eyes and tried to stop thinking about what I wanted to eat for lunch.

... and feel any tension moving out of your body ... as your arms relax ... and notice how your forearms just begin to relax as your hands loosen and let go ... and as you continue to relax your body, notice how your hips and thighs just relax and let go, and the muscles of the shin and calves soften and relax ... that's right ... as your feet sink gently into the earth, feeling them on the ground, relaxing slowly as your whole body just relaxes even more ...

OK, what in the world is happening to me? It's starting to work. For once in my life, my head felt empty.

... and the more you begin to relax, the more your breath goes gently round your body, filling you with relaxing energy ... that's right ... bubbling energetically now ... to the beat of your own heart ... spreading gentle, soothing relaxation through every part of your body ... and you can just let go ... knowing the next time you do this, you can go even deeper.

Pure Zen.

So, as you can imagine, I was proper relaxed. So much so that I might have even started snoring – but before that, I remember having a realisation. It was as if all of my built-up anxieties – about school, my sexuality, July – suddenly fell silent. They had been screaming around my head for so many years, and I was unable to stop them until this moment. Lying on the stinky, cold, dirty floor, surrounded by people I didn't really know, in a place I wasn't familiar with, simply breathing – I finally found a moment's peace. I felt for the first time that things might just get better. I remember tears falling from my eyes on to the floor. It was pure relief. I haven't shared that moment with anyone yet, because I never knew how to explain it, so I hope it made sense. No worries if not.

Right, lets wrap up 2012 and get to the good stuff.

Musical interlude no. 6: 2012

2012's most iconic songs:

'Somebody That I Used to Know' – Gotye
'Payphone' – Maroon 5
'The Motto' – Drake
'Someone Like You' – Adele
'Ass Back Home' – Gym Class Heroes
'Don't Wake Me Up' – Chris Brown
'Climax' – Usher
'I Will Wait' – Mumford & Sons

Iconic things from 2012:

- the first *Hunger Games* film
- everyone being convinced the world was going to end

- Obama being re-elected as US President
- Snoop Dogg changing his name to Snoop Lion
- James Arthur winning *The X Factor*
- Gary Barlow telling Tulisa she had fag ash breath live on *The X Factor*
- Frank getting murdered in Underworld in *Corrie*
- Girls Aloud announcing their iconic TEN Tour

FANGIRLIN' THE HOUSE DOWN BOOTS

So, 2013 was a MOMENT. I was thriving(ish) in college, I went to see Girls Aloud on tour four times, and Cheryl waved at me, twice. I was finally feeling comfortable with myself, in my own skin. My shit haircut was continuing to grow out, and I was slowly learning how to improve my eyebrows. This was also the year I decided to accept that I was very gay, and to let those around me know that I was very gay. Life was getting better – but before we delve further into that, here's another one of my favourite moments from reality TV in poem form:

> I'm sorry to hear that your grandma passed away, yeah?
> I actually am, like, obviously, I'm, I'm going to be upset
> about that, innit, yeah?
> And Hadiqa, you know, the only thing is, yeah, is that no one can force
> me to be your mate or anything, yeah, and I don't want
> to be mates with you, alright.

After a very traumatic, painful and emotional experience of love, I really wasn't looking forward to ever falling in love again. I was more than content being my stupid self, with no worries about who was walking into the canteen and ignoring me, or who wanted to love me one minute and hate me the next (if you're reading this, July, that was a burn *tisssss*). I now associated love with pain – which isn't entirely wrong. I still believe that now: that if you love someone, it'll always cause you pain. If you lose them, it'll hurt. If you argue with them, it'll hurt. If they like someone else's post on Instagram, it might hurt . . . right? I learned from a young age that there is a fine line between love and pain – and love and hate, for that matter. The intensity of love can feel like hate when that person isn't close to us, and if I'm honest, guys, 2013 Soph could not be *fucked* with feeling that all over again. But, in true me-style, that didn't last too long . . . as we'll see.

Anyway, 2013 for me was the year of Twitter. I was so into Twitter; I was tweeting maybe twenty or thirty times a day. All sorts of shite. I was obviously part of the Cheryl fandom, so I spent a lot of my time on there tweeting Cheryl, and crying about it until I got a reply from her. I even have a photo of me literally in floods of tears because she didn't tweet me back. How funny is that? Bless me. I am a sucker for reading back through old messages, tweets, Facebook posts, etc. I love feeling nostalgic. Sometimes when I'm bored, I'll go back through my old tweets from 2009 onwards, and they are something else. I am embarrassed and amused by – and ashamed of – most of them, but in a funny kind of way . . . or maybe I just laugh because that's my way of dealing with any kind of trauma/embarrassment. Who knows?

My entire life was Cheryl, and I made sure everyone knew about it. I don't really know how to best describe a fanbase unless you've been a part of one. I feel like if you haven't, you might just think they're full of weirdos obsessed with a celebrity who couldn't care less about them – and there is a bit of truth in that. However, that wasn't my experience of being in Cheryl's.

Here's a gorgeous explanation of a fanbase from Urban Dictionary:

One of the best and worst parts of having any form of popularity on the internet. This applies to videogames, movies, YouTubers, artists, porn, and basically everything else.

The fanbase is the sum total of all a person's fans, good, bad, and otherwise. While the positive portions of the fanbase often outweigh the negative, it can become irritating for yourself and others when your own fans are constantly harassing another person's fans or each other for essentially no reason.

Fans provide the vital service of spreading your name around for others to hear and come to enjoy your stuff, much in the same way as religious fans never shut up about how you should join their church and talk about their imaginary friend in the sky.

On the other side of this idea, however, you have the fans who spread your work like the crusades, by destroying, demeaning, or getting butthurt over everything/everyone remotely similar to your own work.

It's basically a group of you, usually on Twitter, who spend your entire lives discussing, fantasising about, loving and living for a certain celebrity. To be a part of a fanbase, you would usually fall into the category of a fangirl. I've put together a checklist for you to determine if you are – or ever have been – a fangirl. From Rihanna to *The Vampire Diaries*, don't worry: it's happened to the best of us.

- ☑ You know every single thing about your fave, from their favourite food to what perfume they use, the name of their school and their mother's maiden name.
- ☑ You freak the fuck out when they tweet absolutely anything at all.
- ☑ You are ready to go to prison if anyone says a bad word about them.
- ☑ Your room could be considered an official shrine to them.
- ☑ It's hard to keep your cool when a non-fan mentions them, or when you're out in public and one of their songs comes on.
- ☑ You are obsessed with their fanfiction and cannot stop rereading it.
- ☑ If you ever meet them, or if they tweet you, you literally can't go into school the next day, because you haven't finished hyperventilating.
- ☑ You refer to your fave exclusively by their first name.
- ☑ You ship your fave with another one of your faves.
- ☑ You have met a core group of fangirl friends/girlfriends (in my case) through your fandom and your mutual love of an artist.

- ☑ You experience sheer horror when somebody outside of your fandom finds you on social media.
- ☑ You gently drag your fave from a place of love.
- ☑ 90 per cent of your camera roll is made up of photos of them.
- ☑ You tweet 'dihgfoivjdsOfuwsmsmwregdvnk' in response to *anything* they do.

I know you're wondering what fanfiction is, so let me enlighten you. They can be as short as a sentence, or as long as this book that I'm writing (drink). Fanfiction is a style of amateur fiction, written by fans of a celebrity, a TV show, a book or a film – and it can be about anything at all. I know that One Direction fans like to write stories about Harry and Louis secretly shagging (each to their own) and people go mad for it. I've enjoyed many a lesbian fanfiction in my time; it creates a new reality that you wish was real. Kinda sad, in a happy way. I used to stay up until ungodly hours in the morning reading about an alternate life where Cheryl and Kimberley Walsh were together. A great read: ten out of ten from me. That is what's known as a 'ship' – which is a word to describe your approval of a fictional couple, and can lead to a joint 'shipping name'. For example, Cheryl + Kimberly = Chim. Are you still with me? Good.

There are also different names for different fanbases, some of these you may be familiar with:

Cheryl – Soldiers
One Direction – Directioners
Justin Bieber – Beliebers
Taylor Swift – Swifties
Demi Lovato – Lovatics
Beyoncé – BeyHive
Harry Potter – Potterheads
Rihanna – Navy

I know this will be a lot to take in if you're not familiar with fangirling; and if you are, I know you'll be in your element as you read this.

I've been trying to think of a way to show you the transition from my Cheryl era to my first relationship era. So, here is a tiny collection of my tweets from 2013, which I think are rather telling . . . (Yes, it did take me two whole days to go back through and find these, and yes, I'm embarrassed by some of them, but this is a safe, non-judging space – right?)

January 2013
@SophGalustian SO pissed off. Everyone fuk off
FUCK OFF HOMEWORK I HATE YOU
DO I LOOK LIKE I GIVE A SHIT

February 2013
@SophGalustian I am so stupid
So weird how when you're sad you think you're never gonna stop feeling like shit.
I miss you.

March 2013
@SophGalustian on my way to the MEN to wait 12 hours for the doors to open and if there's any bitch there who thinks they love Cheryl more than me, u don't why the fuck do famous people get to meet other famous people so easily, that is discrimination. How dare Coleen Rooney meet Girls Aloud

April 2013
@SophGalustian woke up and quickly checked Cheryl's profile and she still follows me . . . it wasn't a dream oh my god I can't cope

@SophGalustian I would actually come into physical contact with a spider if it meant that I could meet Cheryl, why the fuck don't I live in London

May 2013

@SophGalustian if there was a word to describe how much I love Cheryl, I'd use it

I'd literally do anything to meet Cheryl, I'd even eat a spider.

does anyone else find it funny the fact that a spider could be a Nanna??

Like it could have baby spiders, who reproduce . . .

June 2013

@SophGalustian in another world, another life, I still belong to you Jessie J sit on my face

living in England is the most boring thing that I've ever had to deal with.

seriously don't know what I'd do without my sister ♥ she does everything for me

July 2013

@SophGalustian WHY have I only just realised where you wee from?!?? CHERYL'S BEEN IN THE STUDIO?!?!?!?! OMFG

why do I have 23 pictures of myself crying on my phone on different occasions?

August 2013

@SophGalustian she can fuck you good but I can fuck you better

can't wait until I'm 18 so I can get out of Manchester and do interesting things with my life

I think I need to learn to be honest with myself before I'm honest with everyone else tbh, hmm this is hard

September 2013

@SophGalustian starting to come to terms with myself

I AM SO GAY

heard my mum downstairs say 'I think Sophs a lesbian, it hurts me that she thinks she can't tell me. Ill love her no matter what'

Im G-A-Y!

October 2013

@SophGalustian It's sooooo weird thinking back to how sad I used to be, & how I always thought it would never change . . .but it did

5 hour FaceTime with ***** was definitely needed 🔫 gonna miss her so much

Couldn't be more in love x

November 2013

@SophGalustian had the most perfect day in the whole world with the most perfect lady. I love my girlfriend <3

SO SO happy

I sometimes just randomly start crying at how happy I am. I can't cope

'you can only find true love when you're true to yourself'

December 2013

@SophGalustian CHERYLS GONNA BE IN CORRIE! CORRIES IN MANCHESTER. I LIVE IN MANCHESTER

Regarding X Factor, nothing will beat Alexandra Burke's duet with Beyoncé

so lucky to have such an amazing, close family. Love them all millions

My girlfriend is my entire world. I love her with my whole heart x

That task taught me that I swore way too much, and that I was obsessed with *Coronation Street*, *The X Factor*, Cheryl and my girlfriend. Yes, you heard me right. My GIRLFRIEND. Allow me to tell you about my second love, who, for the purpose of this book, I will refer to as March.

MARCH (PART ONE)

I have been deep into the Cheryl fanbase since I was around eleven or twelve, and when I finally got Twitter, I became a part of the little community. More or less everyone was gay, even though less than 10 per cent of them had publicly 'come out' back then. I can say it now, because 90 per cent of them have come out over the years, but I also have a very strong gaydar, and I guessed it before everyone else, so . . .

Gaydar: the supposed ability of gay people to recognise one another by means of very subtle indications.

If your gaydar isn't as strong as you'd like it to be, here are some tips for how to gauge if someone might be queer if you're too scared to ask. (These are based on my opinions only, please and thank you.)

1. **Talk about what she's watching.** This is such a telling conversation topic. If she's into *Killing Eve*, *Bly Manor*, *Ratched*, *Disobedience* and *Drag Race*, she's probably gay. Observe and see if she gets enthusiastic over them. Lord knows we gays are all over any film or storyline with a hint of LGBTQ+.
2. **What shoes is she wearing?** Converse, Vans, Docs, Birks and Crocs all scream 'gay' to me. If you're a high femme reading this, you're excused. Keep wearing your heels.
3. **Ask her where she likes to go out.** See if it's an LGBTQ+ venue. I usually say something like, 'I don't really enjoy normal clubs, the men piss me off.' However, I've learned over time that this isn't an exclusively gay sentiment: my straight friends feel exactly the same way.
4. **What music is she into?** Christine and the Queens? If so, you're probably on to a winner.
5. **Does she have a cat?** Again, not foolproof, but extremely common. Same with lots of plants in her room.
6. **If you're comfortable doing so, casually out yourself in a conversation.** If she's queer, she may do the same.
7. **Check out her nails.** Most lesbians will have immaculately clean, short nails. They are our trademark, after all.

You could also ask if she's part of a fanbase. In my personal opinion, you have to have at least a tiny bit of gay in you to dedicate your entire life to a hot female celebrity.

There was a handful of girls in our Twitter fanbase who I thought were fit, and one of those girls was March. I tweeted her in January 2012 saying, 'Hey please can you follow me back ☺ xx', which is not only embarrassing, but tragic. What made it worse was that she IGNORED that tweet and didn't follow me back. Ouch.

But in true me-style, I was persistent. I knew she was gay from the outset, because she'd tweet relentlessly about how sexy girls were and how repulsed she was by men. So, I didn't even need to engage my gaydar; she did all the work for me. I had developed an enormous crush on her, and the more she ignored me, the more I fancied her. I think this may have been deeply rooted in the way that I couldn't stop loving July, even though she sometimes rejected me – if anything, it made me want her more. So, I had established that I enjoyed the chase. I am a confident person anyway, as you might have gathered, so I saw it as a challenge to get March to really see me for who I was, not just a strange Cheryl fan who cries when Cheryl tweets her.

Once, March tweeted about thinking septum piercings were sexy, and lo and behold, I had my septum pierced. This was a perfect opportunity to show myself. So, I somehow had the guts to reply to her tweet with a sexy (and edited) photo of me with my septum piercing. My heart was pounding in my chest; my bum was pulsing. I was nervous for her response. It . . . didn't happen. She AIRED my tweet. Can you imagine the sheer embarrassment that caused me? I nearly deleted my account. She literally ignored it and carried on tweeting as if it hadn't happened. I was so burned. The only reason I didn't delete my account was because Cheryl followed it.

So, I took a step back, and attempted my 'hard-to-get' phase. This is something I never ever have been, and never ever will be, successful at. I'm too much, like a maniacal Labrador. I couldn't be mysterious if I tried. I continued to like her tweets, sometimes. To let her know I was still around, and sexy. She eventually liked a selfie of mine, and I nearly threw myself out of the window with excitement. That was the start of our flirting phase.

3 September 2013. 18:18.
Soph: Don't think I'm weird but you were in my dream last night . . .x
3 September 2013. 18:21.
March: ha ha, really? what happened? x

We didn't end up going to sleep until 5am after this conversation. We spoke on Twitter all night, into the early hours, and eventually exchanged numbers. We just automatically clicked, and had so much to talk about. I remember lying in bed and being so giddy to be talking to her, because I'd fancied her for so long that it felt like a reward being able to chat with her the way I was. The rest was history, literally. We spoke every single day after that; we'd FaceTime for seven or eight hours at a time. Sometimes we'd fall asleep on FaceTime, and I'd wake up and she'd still be there. Sleeping very peacefully.

March is from London, so I couldn't just nip and meet her for a drink, which made things very emotional. I think it was also the start of my 'I love London' era (another phase of Soph on Twitter). In a matter of months, we had shared all of our secrets, had endless phone calls, and confessed our love for one another, all before even meeting in person. My mum would often come into my room and say, 'Who are you on the phone to?' I told her it was March. A 'friend'. Lol. I was planning to go down to London to see her for the first time, and I was so incredibly nervous. March comes from a very sheltered, safe and loved home. A bit like the one I described at the start of this book (drink) where everyone has matching John Lewis PJs and the floor is covered with thick carpets. Her life was very different to mine, and I wanted to put my best self forward so that she still liked me. This makes me sad now, because I shouldn't have felt that I needed to pretend to be something I wasn't in order to impress someone, but she was really lovely, so don't judge me.

I saved up my dinner money from college, which was still going great, FYI. I used this money to buy myself some brand-new Timberland boots for £85. I didn't wear them until our date, when I used the classic line, 'Oh, I've had these ages,' despite the fact they were fresh out of the box and I'd starved for a couple of months in order to buy them. I also robbed a long-sleeved top from Primark. It was black and grey, and I spent all evening with Danny unpicking the 'Cedar Wood State' label from the back so March wouldn't know that I shopped in – or in this case, stole from – Primark. This makes me laugh my head off now, because when I eventually told her, she's such a different class from me that she didn't even know what Cedar Wood was.

I eventually booked a coach down to London to see her. It was a five-hour journey, and I spent the entire time listening to 'Adore You' by Miley Cyrus. It was 2 November 2013. I remember seeing her for the first time at London Victoria station. She was so beautiful, and a lot tinier than I'd thought she'd be. To be able to hug her and have her in my arms after what literally felt like a lifetime of waiting was just pure magic – and she smelled like actual heaven too. As I've mentioned, I've always had a thing for nice smells. We went to the cinema to see *Cloudy with a Chance of Meatballs*, which we watched for approximately seven minutes before snogging for the rest of the film. The next day, we went to the aquarium, and I nearly passed out because I needed a poo so badly, and I didn't go for two days because I obviously couldn't let her know that I shit. So I was literally bent double walking around, and I had to tell her it was period pains – which, again, makes me laugh so much now. I think I went white and looked really poorly, and she was genuinely worried about me. Moral of the story: do not hold in your bodily functions! It's a lot more painful than you might think . . .(I know a lot of people that don't do normal human things in front of people they like. Gemma never used to eat in front of her boyfriends, and I used to say to them, 'Gemma was just eating, but she's stopped now because you're here.' I was always dropping her in it.)

Anyway, I left after the weekend, and I felt so happy and so in love with March. It was the first time since July that I'd had strong feelings for somebody else, and it was a relief, because I had convinced myself that I would never love anybody again. March was my second love. Very different to my first, but very deep and very strong, nevertheless. Nothing was comparable to July. Apparently, your second love teaches you how to love again after you've been broken. They teach you that you're capable of loving again and being loved. It's not based on obsession and it isn't blind; you are in a better headspace for making decisions and avoiding getting hurt. March taught me that I deserved to be loved, and also that I deserved to be happy and at peace with myself and my sexuality. So, I know you're now probably thinking, how did I come out? Well, let me tell ya . . .

I'M COMING OUT

While we're on the subject of 'coming out', I should tell you that I fucking *hate* it as a concept. I hate it because I think it adds an unnecessary pressure on top of an already heightened and potentially scary situation. And I hate it the most because it's one of the reasons that July and I didn't get our 'happily ever after' at that time. The social pressure of concealing or revealing your sexual and/or gender identity is such a complex and challenging process – and why should we, the wonderful gays, have to go through that if the straights don't? Very unfair, if you ask me. I do, however, think people view coming out differently. Some people view it as a process. Often, the first step is coming out to yourself, self-acceptance, which allows you to progress to the next stage of telling those around you.

Although I had always known I was gay, I don't think I had accepted it within myself. It's like, inside my head I knew it, but I wouldn't allow it to become my reality for a long time – until it did become my reality, like when I got a girlfriend. I was ashamed of being ashamed of myself; I guess I was just scared to accept myself, which caused me to project those fears on to the people around me, as if they wouldn't be accepting.

I have had numerous conversations about it, and I've done a lot of research into 'coming out' as a concept, and I really don't agree with a lot of the things I've read. Some people say, 'Give those around you time to adjust to this new information.' If I'm totally honest, that just fucks me off? Why do *they* need time to adjust to *my* sexual preferences? That's my business, not theirs.

I think I can be like a bomb waiting to go off around the subject, because of how much it's affected me and my relationships over the years, and because I've seen people who I love struggling with it, too. I truly believe that if the people around you love you, they won't even blink at your sexuality, because, realistically, what does it matter? My best friend is straight, and I don't care for that way of life. However, I love her regardless of this – it's as simple as that. If the people around you respond in a way that makes you uncomfortable or upset, well, that sounds like a *them* problem, not a *you* problem. We're out here trying to live a happy life, loving who we want to love. If others have an issue with that, they are clearly unhappy and/or bored with their own lives, and are trying to project their unhappiness on to us. Believe me, life is too short to be damned with that kind of energy, especially from the very people who are supposed to love and uplift us. These are my opinions, which I have developed over my years of being openly gay and comfortable within myself.

So, if you're reading this and you're feeling overwhelmed, or if you're asking yourself why you don't feel this strongly about it – don't panic. It's a journey that you'll go on, and that journey looks different for every single person. This is just mine.

I didn't always have these views. At first, I was obviously scared, and catastrophised every single possible outcome. As you get older, though, I think you just stop caring what others think of you, and you discover that your happiness needs to be protected at all costs, whatever that happiness may look like.

It's also important to acknowledge that other people may not have a safe environment in which to explore their sexuality, and nobody deserves to be shamed if they are still living in the closet. You have no idea what goes on in other people's personal lives; you can only support them in whatever way you can until they're safe enough to be open. Coming out should be about celebrating the beauty of being true to yourself, and having the courage to share an important part of your life with others. It should not be perceived as 'exposing' yourself or 'confessing' something. It's simply part of your identity. In an ideal world being straight and/or cis wouldn't be considered the default, and nobody would make assumptions about anyone else's sexual orientation or gender identity. I hope that one day, we can stop living in such a binary world of titles and labels, and just do whatever the fuck makes us happy.

If you are seeking support for acknowledging, exploring, or accepting your sexuality, here are some starting points:

- Talk to other LGBTQ+ people who may share their experiences of coming out.
- Join online communities of LGBTQ+ people (Twitter is a good place to start).
- Talk to trusted LGBTQ+ adults who you may already know, such as family members or teachers.
- LGBTQ+ organisations such as Stonewall have great support forums.

So, I guess I should share my 'coming out' story. I should note that my close friends at the time knew I was gay, but I didn't even have to tell them. Gemma guessed when we were in school, because she could tell I was in love with July, and Danny always knew, because he has a great gaydar.

During my weekend in London with March, I had asked her to be my girlfriend on the Tube (very romantic, I know). I remember just looking at her and counting to ten in my head, and thinking, *Just say it, just say it*. So I took a deep breath and said, 'So, are you my girlfriend now then?' That was my cool way of asking. She smiled and said yes, and we both laughed. I knew then that I would need to tell my mum, so that March could come and visit and not be seen as my 'friend'. I planned to tell Mum the next day. Danny said he'd come with me so I wasn't as scared or embarrassed.

So, here is an exact replica of what I said to my mum and how she responded:

Me: Come back early tomoz please I wanna talk to you xxxxx

Mum: Ok well have a great night. Talk to me???? Now you've got me worried lol. Don't be leaving home yet you're not allowed. If it's about your inner feelings I have known for yrs and I don't care and any prejudice from anyone else will have me to answer to. If it's not that and you're pregnant then fuck that don't want any more grandkids lol. Only joking. Love you soooooo much and miss you. Xxxxxxx

When mums say they 'just know' things, they really do. How on earth did my mum know from that text that I wanted to talk about my 'inner feelings'?! I understand she might have had a slight inkling from earlier signs, such as my dyke haircut and the fact I was madly obsessed with a female popstar, or the way I didn't ever answer the door to my boyfriends . . . but the fact she knew from just that text was pretty weird. Her response helped me relax a lot, but when it got to it, I just sat on the sofa in silence, because I was still scared. My mum looked at me and said, 'I know and I love you.' She gave me a massive hug, and that was literally it.

I realise how lucky I am to have received that response from her, and I feel very grateful to be surrounded by people who love me and support me. I left it up to my mum to tell most of the rest of my family, because I just couldn't be arsed, to be honest. I didn't see the big deal, really, but I wanted them to know that March was my girlfriend. I think I might have told Stacey myself; she was obviously completely fine with it.

My mum told my nanny, who was ninety-three at the time. I was a bit worried about her reaction, to be honest, because some old people have backwards views. I don't excuse their views because they're old, by the way; I don't think that's a valid excuse for being racist, sexist or homophobic. Times are constantly changing around us; if someone has outdated and harmful thoughts, it's their own responsibility to change that. It isn't down to us to excuse them. Anyway, Nanny's response was, 'Well, the most important thing in this life is love, and if you've found it, don't ever let it go.' That makes me want to weep. What a beautiful thing to say to me. She was born in 1922, so whenever somebody tries to justify an old person saying something offensive or harmful, I think of her and I just can't accept it. My nanny lived through a time when it was illegal to be gay, when black people couldn't marry white people, when women

152

weren't treated as human beings – and that didn't mean she lived her life agreeing with those things. We are all responsible for our own thoughts and judgements; it doesn't matter where or how you grew up, or how old you are. You can change if you want to – and if you don't want to, you are the only person to blame.

And that leads me on to the next person I was scared to tell. My dad. I didn't tell my dad until March and I had been together for three years (spoiler). I know that's wild, but I didn't see him often enough for him to know the ins and outs of my life, so it was easy to conceal it. The reason I feared telling him was because he was born and raised in Iran, where it's still illegal to be gay, and death by stoning is permitted – live, love, laugh, y'all. I guess I was worried that my dad might share those harmful views, and I was too scared to find out, because I love him so much I didn't want it to change how I viewed him. He eventually came into my room one day and saw I had a huge Pride flag pinned to my wall (obviously, why wouldn't I?). He asked what it was, despite knowing full well . . . I told him it was a Pride flag, and he said, 'Oh, OK.' I ended up telling him that night, and he cried. He cried because he was upset I'd felt as though I needed to keep it from him. He told me that he loved me no matter what, and he wished I could have felt able to tell him sooner. It was the biggest relief. He did say he'd always known; he'd just been waiting for me to be ready to share it. All of which reiterates what I mentioned before, about it not mattering where or how you grew up; you are in charge of your own views and it is as simple as that. This next one is called 'Proud'.

We owe our freedom to our LGBTQ+ family.
They have paved the way for us to exist today.
I'm going to take it back to 1969:
the start of the rise of our time.
If you were gay, you were nothing but the enemy.
Described as mentally ill, sick in the head.
You'd be lucky to survive and not end up dead.

You'd be sent to a camp of conversion, to try and heal you of
your 'perversion',
so they called it.
The original LGBT flag was hand-dyed and consisted of eight symbolic
colours
to represent all the gay, oppressed lovers.
Pride is being proud of who we are, despite facing discrimination daily
and then some.
So, before you ask why there isn't a straight Pride, be thankful you don't
need one.
I personally believe I was born gay.
It has always been a part of my DNA.
Growing up, I was made to feel disgusted by who I liked.
'You fancy women? And you're a woman . . . that's not alright.'
My search history would consist of *'How to be straight'*.
I can't feel feelings for him, nothing more than a mate.
I tried so hard, I'd get myself into a state.
I just needed to learn how to communicate what I was feeling.
How to let go of the part of myself I was concealing.
I was cramped in the closest, it was unappealing.
I'm ready to share, I'm ready to reveal it.
I grew up believing *lesbian* was a dirty word.
Hearing of same-sex female couples was unheard.
Our love interests result in us being physically attacked.
That isn't dramatic or fabricated, it's actual facts.
I think it's crazy that who I love pisses off so many people.
Is it too much to ask to just be equal?
Straight couples will be snogging at the back of the bus,
while I can't even hold my girlfriend's hand without attracting a fuss.
The whispers and glares, I know I shouldn't care, but it happens
everywhere.
If I had £1 for each time, I'd be a fuckin' millionaire.

Are you ignorant or just unaware? You're making me uncomfortable,
like I shouldn't be there.
Didn't your mum ever teach you that its rude to stare?
In reality, you homophobes are the so-called 'perverts'.

I don't want to be straight any more,
I don't want to convert.
Don't forget that Pride is a protest.
We are oppressed.
We will fight for equality until the end,
we won't rest.
I've learned to be proud of who I am,
to take pride in being gay because I can.
And to every non-binary person, or self-identifying woman or man,
never forget how Pride began:
Marsha P. Johnson,
a Black trans woman.

HERE'S SOME SPACE FOR YOU TO REFLECT ON
THIS SECTION. I KNOW IT MIGHT HAVE BEEN
HEAVY.

Right, let's wrap up 2013, shall we? I do think the music got shitter as time went on. For me, nothing will beat 2007–2012, but maybe that's because I just can't move on from that time of my life. Things also became less iconic generally, especially once Cheryl left *The X Factor*. So let's just stick to songs going forward. (I also stopped watching the soaps in 2013. I know, shock horror, but guys, I did have a gf, so shaggin' took priority.)

Musical interlude no. 7: 2013

Iconic songs from 2013:

'Just Hold On, We're Going Home' – Drake
'Stay' – Rihanna feat. Mikky Ekko
'Royals' – Lorde
'I Knew You Were Trouble' – Taylor Swift
'We Can't Stop' – Miley Cyrus
'Holy Grail' – Jay-Z feat. Justin Timberlake
'Clarity' – Zedd feat. Foxes
'Same Love' – Macklemore & Ryan Lewis feat. Mary Lambert
'Adorn' – Miguel
'Fuckin' Problems' – A$AP Rocky feat. Drake, Kendrick Lamar and 2 Chainz

HAVE YOU BEEN IN AN ACCIDENT THAT WASN'T YOUR FAULT?

Apart from it being my last year at college, 2014 felt like a relatively quiet year. I feel like my entire life at that point was made up of March and Cheryl. People in my class had started looking at universities and drama schools, and if I'm honest with you, that wasn't what I wanted at that point. It makes me cringe even typing this now, but I was genuinely convinced that I was *that* good, I didn't *need* to go on to higher education.

I thought that as soon as I left college, I'd be snapped up by a big Hollywood director (not sure why a Hollywood director would be in Salford, but nevertheless). I obviously went on to learn the hard way that this wouldn't be the case, and that I would, in fact, end up working harder than those around me and still get nowhere. I still hadn't let March come to my house yet. My mum had a boyfriend at the time who lived in a massive house in Gatley (bit posh, had a porch), so I used to bring her there instead, because obviously my house was being 'redecorated'. The first time she stayed over, we made pizzas. It was the first time I'd ever done that in my life, but I wanted her to think we were wholesome like that; we even got the ingredients from Sainsbury's instead of Morrisons.

I much preferred going to her place in London. I tried my first avocado there – I pretended that I'd had them loads of times before and that I loved them, but if I'm honest, I didn't even know what an avocado was before going to her house. It was exciting to get out of Manchester for a bit and experience different things.

While juggling my first relationship and dedicating my life to a celebrity, I somehow managed a D*D*D at college. I should say, I had a great time at college. If I compare it to the unhappiness I felt at school, college was an actual dream, both because I was doing something that I loved every day, and because I had this new inner acceptance. By this point, my peers were being accepted into some of the top drama schools and universities in the UK. I had left it too late to even start thinking that could be a possibility, so I brushed it off and would say things like, 'Aw, I'm not gonna bother with drama school, me.' My teacher at the time would give me a certain look that I never understood. I get it now. It was the look of, *You are going to have the shock of your life* – and they were absolutely right. I think Michelle Keegan went to my college, and I used to think I'd probably follow in her footsteps: secure a nice role in *Corrie*, and bosh. Sorted.

They really hammered it into us at college how difficult the industry was, and how we had a less than 1 per cent chance of being successful. I always found this demotivating and negative, and I didn't understand why they would say it, but I know now they were just trying to prepare us for an industry that was not only difficult to crack, but that had no room for, or interest in, working-class kids with no money. So, I did what every lost seventeen-year-old does. I took a year out.

I'd like to say I went travelling during this year, and spent it bathing endangered elephants in Thailand and living off coconuts while being admired by the sexy locals and flooding my Instagram page with photos of sunsets and six-packs, and doing boomerangs of my $3 pad Thai that I bought from a street market. Instead, I got a job in the world's most soul-destroying call centre, spending every day cold-calling innocent people to discuss hypothetical road-traffic accidents that they may or may not have had in the last twenty years, and slyly trying to convince them that their minor bump at 5 miles per hour had in fact given them whiplash. It was dehumanising. Some people can absolutely smash those jobs and make a lot of cash; usually, those people are motivated entirely by money and are not controlled by their conscience – or perhaps they don't even have one. That was *not* me. Obviously, I wanted money but I didn't want it enough to compromise the part of my brain that makes me feel guilt. I would genuinely be close to tears trying to convince OAPs to commit fraud, basically. It was never sold as that to us, of course. It was very much put across that *we* would be doing *them* a favour. Why wouldn't they want to claim £4,000 that they may be entitled to? But I am led by my conscience, and it never felt good pushing people into that. I know that might sound really dramatic, and you might be reading that thinking, *Oh, shut the fuck up, mard arse, and make some money.* And I get that, I do. I am just not built for that role. I don't like being pushy.

What I'm trying to tell you is I was absolutely shite at that job. I would end up talking to people about their lives instead, and the weather, or how their holiday was that they'd recently come back from. I once helped a woman change her TV to HDMI 2 over the phone, and I explained to a man that you can make eggs in the microwave. I even talked him through how to make them fluffy, step by step. Bit of milk, bit of butter. One minute in, gentle stir, another thirty seconds, then sprinkle with pepper. My manager bollocked me and said that I spent too much time chatting and not enough time putting through claims, but hey, I was great at building a strong rapport. Just not very great at making money. I was accepting of that. Can't be good at *everything*, jeez.

It was sort of my first proper job with a steady wage. It was £12,000 a year basic, which at the time I thought was amazing, bless me. The people around me were making £20,000-plus, easy, because they were good at the job and were making commission. I guess it wasn't too bad for me, because I was still living at home and didn't really have any commitments apart from giving my mum rent every month, which she spent on food and wine. (As an adult now, I can totally relate.)

Musical interlude no. 8: 2014

Here are some iconic songs to wrap up 2014:

'Happy' – Pharrell Williams
'Waves' – Mr Probz
'Stay With Me' – Sam Smith
'Nobody To Love' – Sigma
'Uptown Funk' – Mark Ronson feat. Bruno Mars
'Crazy Stupid Love' – Cheryl
'Drunk in Love' – Beyoncé
'Pompeii' – Bastille
'Dark Horse' – Katy Perry

A HARDWORKING, COMPASSIONATE AND DEDICATED INDIVIDUAL

Working at that call centre knocked my confidence, big time. Don't get me wrong; when I wasn't forcing whiplash down people's throats, people would always tell me how kind I was on the phone. That made me feel good, but kindness wasn't going to make me a successful actor or writer. I had these massive dreams of being successful and rich – and none of them aligned with what I was currently doing. I would sometimes look around at my colleagues who were a lot older than me and think, *Fuck*. They were earning decent money, but they looked unhappy. I needed to get out. I can understand how people can get stuck in dead-end jobs, because they get comfortable, and it's reliable, and they have a steady wage. I feared that I was falling into that hole, with my big girl wage of £12k.

(I hope you've not taken any offence to me referring to a call centre as a dead-end job; I understand that for some people it isn't, and they're comfortable with that role, and I respect that entirely. Good for you, if you're enjoying it and you're happy to be there. I know some people excel in those roles and are built for making commission and chasing money goals. I am envious of those people. I just had different goals that I'd convinced myself I would achieve, and this job was an obstacle to those goals.)

I believed in myself too much to make do. So, I started to panic. I watched my peers from college finish their first years at drama school, posting pictures in their black clothes with their scripts and their Chilly's water bottles. I ate my words, and started looking at universities. I would have preferred to go to drama school over university, but I had convinced myself that I wouldn't fit in, because only rich, privileged kids with famous mums go there. (I later learned this wasn't entirely true, but also wasn't entirely false.) I would often discourage myself from attending certain places because of an internalised fear that I wouldn't fit in or wouldn't be good enough. I wish I'd just run into those situations head-first, which I did go on to do a bit later in life.

While unenthusiastically surfing the UCAS website, I learned quickly that there was going to be an issue with me getting into university. As you may recall from earlier, not only did I not pass my Maths GCSE, but I took a hard fail. I know what you're thinking: why the *fuck* do you need maths to do an acting course? Honestly, fuck knows. But you did, and I was staring to panic even more.

I was only looking at universities in London, because I'd developed an obsession with it and March lived there, so naturally, I wanted to be closer to her while acquiring £27,000 of debt – every cloud. Reluctantly, my first choice was Kingston University. This was purely because it was close to March and looked very grassy and peaceful. March encouraged this; I guess she thought I might not throw up through my nose and attend foam parties like at a more rural uni. Luckily, I didn't get in, because of Maths – never thought I'd say this but, thank fuck for Maths. That's a great example of why things happen for a reason. If I had gone to Kingston, I might not even be writing this book (DRINK!). I don't think everything happens for a reason, FYI. I used to, until my nephew died. I don't believe there was any reason for that. Why would there be? I mean, it's made me apathetic, non-empathetic and depressed, so . . .

One too many words for me; let's mix it up with another one of my favourite reality-TV moments:

JANE

Oh, oh, why are you shaking your head at me?

PETER

You won, Jane. Enjoy the money.

JANE

Oh my god. Oh my god.

PETER

I hope it makes you happy. Dear lord, what a sad little life, Jane. You ruined my night completely so you could have the money, but I hope now you can spend it on lessons in grace and decorum, because you have all the grace of a reversing dump truck without any tyres on.

CHARLOTTE

Hmm, I don't get it.

PETER

Well, you wouldn't. Let's be honest, there's nobody in there, love. So, Jane, take your money and get off my property.

My second choice of university was London South Bank. These are the reasons why I chose it, in order:

- close to March
- close to the London Eye
- red buses are cool
- the course seemed OK.

I searched long and hard in my emails for the personal statement I sent in with my application. I don't know how I feel about this, but I found it, so yes, I'm going to include it – with some annotations:

I am a hardworking, compassionate and dedicated individual. I am a strong believer in motivating myself and others to create an atmosphere that allows us to work productively. Through experience, I have learned that to be able to adapt to any role I am given, I need to be empathetic and open-minded. This has influenced me both on- and off-stage, which has helped me achieve success in my academic and personal life. *(So over-said.)*

In high school, I took part in class productions, which allowed me to discover my flexibility within performing. My confidence and desire for performing has just continued to grow throughout my life and this reflects on my audience. From a young age I have been able take criticism positively and allow it to aid me in becoming a better performer. *(Completely untrue; I would cry if people told me I wasn't good.)* For GCSE, I played an eighteen-year-old German girl in a production called 'The White Rose'. I was able to engage in my role both physically and emotionally as I researched the historical aspect of this character, this helped me to empathise and perform effectively. *(Bullshit.)* I am a keen team player and was given responsibility to lead the group, which included planning rehearsals and warm-up activities.

In Pendleton we performed various scripts for assessments, all of which were very different; we covered a wide range of modules from Film to Physical Theatre. We also studied various practitioners, such as Sanford Meisner, Stanislavski and Bertolt Brecht. *(Couldn't tell you one thing about any of these practitioners now.)* This was interesting because I could get an insight into how different methods were used. I enjoyed studying different aspects of drama. I did find some modules challenging at times, but this motivated me to work harder.

For our final performance, we took on Edward Bond's 'Saved'. The script was an unforgettable and shocking play to read as it was originally refused a licence without severe cuts by Lord Chamberlain. *(I copied and pasted that part from Google; I don't even know what it means.)* I was given the character of 'Pam', who was a poverty stricken, young mother which further reinforces my diversity in drama. *(Lmfao.)* After we did the performance in college, we were awarded to perform it at the Lowry Theatre in central Manchester, which was open to the general public and a fantastic experience.

After completing my course, I wanted to experience working in an adult environment and put what I've learned in communication into practice. My role consists of talking to over 100 different people on the phone, processing claims and taking inbound complaints. *(Aka cold-calling and committing fraud.)* This has improved my listening skills as it enables me to communicate with a very wide variety of people. *(No, it didn't. It left me riddled with anxiety and unhappiness.)* It's taught me about the importance of working individually under pressure, and as part of a team.

Aside from acting, I very much enjoy singing. I feel very confident with my acting abilities. I haven't yet found the same level of confidence in singing, however this is an area I'd like to develop further with the right support if given the opportunity. *(Embarrassing and just not true.)* I have taken part in many fundraisers such as a twelve-mile sponsored walk for charities such as St Ann's Hospice, Cancer Research and Water Aid. *(We were literally forced to do this in school. It wasn't a choice, and I don't think it was even those charities.)* An acting agency called Lime Management have been in contact with me after running a workshop at my college and would like me to attend further workshops with them, which I think will be great experience in my year out, and to keep my 'acting muscles' working, as my tutor used to say. *(I didn't go.)* Also, I am joining some close friends of mine in attending an acting workshop once a week for two hours called 'Actors Lab'. *(This was a lie.)*

I feel that my passion for performing and my enthusiasm for gaining more knowledge on the subject has driven me to pursue Drama at university. I have faith that this will open many doors for me to achieve my future career as a performer. Having done drama from a young age, *('done drama')* I have been able to adjust to any role as I am capable of becoming a blank canvas in order to portray my character successfully, which I believe is vital to complete this course to the best of my ability. *(Very GCSE chat here.)*

After a stressful UCAS application and a heavily plagiarised, bullshit-padded personal statement, lo and behold: I got accepted. I was still unsure if I even wanted to go at this point, I just knew I couldn't spend another minute in that hellish call centre. So, uni seemed like the better option.

I used to think you had to be very clever and/or posh and rich to attend uni. I was the first person in my family to be accepted. Now it feels like more people are succeeding without higher education, which is great. If you can save yourself debt, depression and anaemia, then I would recommend doing so.

The plus side of being poor with a divorced mum and dad and living in a council gaff was that I was entitled to the highest amount of student loan and grant, which would just about carry me through. I had managed to save a couple of grand from my shit job, too, so I was all set to go and start my new journey. Obviously, I wouldn't know anybody in London apart from March, but I'd had no issue with that in college. I would miss my family and friends in Manchester, of course, but I'm pretty decent at making new friends, and the thought of the fresh start was thrilling. I loved the idea of going somewhere and nobody knowing anything about me, so they could form fresh opinions and not judge me on the fact that I lied myself into an ambulance in 2008, you know?

Uni

STUDENT LIFE

My family thought it was proper cool that I was going to London; so did my mates. Some people asked why I had chosen London, and I couldn't tell them it was to be closer to March, because they'd say I was fuckin' daft, so I'd say something like, 'There's more to life than Manchester.' How annoying of me.

Although they were happy for me, my family were sad to learn that I was moving away. Especially my dad, as I am the only person in this country he has, but we came to an agreement that I would ring him every single day – and I am glad to tell you that I did. My mum was happy for me, and actually made the decision to move to Portugal when I moved to London. She'd always wanted to live abroad: the lifestyle is better, it's sunny and the wine is cheap. She obviously couldn't go when I was at home, so what a perfect time to follow her dreams at the same time as I was following mine. If mum had gone to Portugal while I was still at home, I would not have coped without her. However, with me moving away, it seemed like a good time for her to go and do what she wanted! I still missed her so much, but being in London occupied my mind. Of course, Mum moving to Portugal meant that even if I wanted to change my mind and go back home to my bedroom, I physically couldn't. As it would no longer be there.

I remember the journey down to London with Stacey and Mum; I was really excited, and oddly not feeling very sad. Obviously, that sadness then hit me hard after they left, but I really felt ready for this new chapter. Even though I hadn't particularly wanted to go to university, I was willing to give it my all. Still, in the back of my mind, I was convinced I'd probably do half a year to a year there, before landing my dream role and dropping out. I hadn't grown out of that delusional phase just yet.

So, I arrived in London in one piece. March met me at my student accommodation to help me unpack and get settled. I went to the front desk to pay my deposit of £4,000. I think the cost of the room was around £160 a week, which seems extortionate – and I'm here to tell you that it was.

It was the tiniest, dampest, smelliest room I'd ever been in, and I couldn't believe I was about to pay that amount of money to sleep on a bed that was about as comfortable as sleeping on a Yellow Pages. My wooden desk had the world 'HELL' engraved on the side, and the 'en suite' had silver fish. Home sweet home. It was shit, but it was *my* shit. I put up some photos of the people I loved – Mum, Dad, Stacey, Matthew, Luke, Emily, Nanna and Nanny – and unpacked my entire life. And that was me.

I had been given so many books on 'student life' and what to expect. I even printed out a massive checklist of the advice that had been given to me prior to moving. Based on that and my own experiences, I would suggest the following:

- Get a railcard.
- Download every single money-saving app that exists.
- Apply student discount to everything you possibly can.
- Bring things from home to get your room feeling as cosy as possible.
- Bring lots of medicine, because you will get sick within the first few months.
- Register with a GP ASAP, because you will need to go within the first few months.
- Buy food that doesn't go off easily; lots of cupboard stuff.
- Go to Tesco and get one of those massive bags of pasta.
- Learn to cook something basic, like pasta.
- Manage your money well, unless your family are rich and will always bail you out.

- Only buy or bring cheap stuff for the kitchen. Other people will use it, not wash it and/or break it.
- Do not join every society. You will not attend them.
- Don't settle for the first person you meet. You will meet lots of people.
- Never do a food shop when you're hungry. You don't need those Rolo yogurts.
- Never put your colours in with your whites when doing a wash.
- Learn the difference between best-before and use-before sell-by dates.
- Accept that you are, and will be, feeling homesick.
- Don't buy your reading list brand new; always get the shitty second-hand copies.
- Keep your moving-in boxes; you'll need them when you move out. Duh.

I learned a lot of the above the hard way. Like when I joined the Jujitsu Society and the Cheese Society, and they both held meetings on the same day at the same time. Very stressful! So in true me-style, I ignored every email I got until they both eventually left me alone.

I like having nice, clean things and spaces around me. I think it's because I didn't have that a lot as a kid, so it's important for me to have it as an adult. So I kept my tiny, shit room spotless, and I was always cleaning the kitchen after the animals that were my flatmates had messed it up. Why is it always the rich kids who are so fucking messy and don't wash their hair?

I also kept money saved constantly. I would decline nights out because I didn't want to spend my money on that, and some of my friends would be £1,000-plus into their overdrafts, calling me boring and uptight about money. Which is hilarious, because their mums and dads could afford to bail them out of literally anything; mine couldn't. I think that's why I started to look after my money, because I knew if I blew it, I would have nothing and nobody to fall back on. I was on my own in that regard. Ultimately, that has taught me a lot, and I'm thankful, but before you start judging other people on how they save or spend their money, check your own privileges first. Here's why you shouldn't question other people's finances:

- *It's none of your business.*

NORTH AND SOUTH

Aside from adapting to university life, I was also adapting to living in a completely different part of the country. It took moving out of the north for me to realise that we are very different from the south – and when I say different, I mean better. We're better than the south. If you're reading this and you're southern, I'm sorry, but your tap water tastes like shite. I'm kidding. (Not about the water – that really *is* bad.) In all seriousness, though, there really is a great divide. Some of the differences are just generally funny or even fictional, but others are real differences in our cultures and attitudes.

So, I'm sure you're wondering, what are the differences that divide the north and the south? What quirks are unique to us northerners? Allow me to explain.

- Northerners will speak to strangers, willingly. When you get on the Tube in London, everyone – and I mean *everyone* – has their head in their phone or a newspaper. If you dared to utter a word, you would be exiled. Once, I was in a queue to top up my Oyster card, and I turned to the lady behind me and said, 'Bloody 'ell, be here all day at this rate.' She literally just stared at me blankly and didn't say a word. Didn't even crack a smile. It doesn't need to be a stimulating conversation; it can be as simple as, 'Freezing today, innit?' This concept is very alien to a southerner.
- We have shit weather in the north. The saying 'it's grim up north' really is true. I didn't realise how cold it was in the north until I went to London and discovered that the southern definition of 'freezing' is actually very mild. Also, they're mard arses over a bit of rain. To a northerner, anything above ten degrees with sun is beer-garden weather.
- Northerners will always view southerners as 'posh'. Doesn't matter which part of the south you're from, or what your socio-economic background is; to us, you're soft.
- I needed to take out a payday loan after I bought my first round of drinks in London.

- This sounds obvious, but we speak differently. I'd always thought my accent was tame, until I moved down south and everyone compared me to Peter Kay. Most of the time, I had to say things twice in order to be understood. Southerners particularly enjoyed hearing me say the words 'grass' or 'bath'.
- Southerners reckon they love footy, but we are completely football-mad up north. It's not just a sport, it's literally a way of life. Once my cousin had a boyfriend who was a United fan, and my uncle didn't let him in the house. It's literally that deep.
- This one is slightly stereotyped, but northerners do enjoy gravy with most things. Especially chips. Once, when I got in from a night out and I was absolutely fucked and starving, I ate an entire bowl of Bisto with bread. I don't regret it. The first chippy I went to in London didn't even sell gravy or curry sauce, and it cost me £4.50 for a portion of small chips. They weren't even crispy. Fuming.
- In the north, we will refer to complete strangers with terms of endearment. Usually 'love' or 'pet'. We're friendly like that. I will always say, 'Cheers love,' when I'm in Manchester but I would *never* in London; I couldn't cope with the backlash.
- Northerners are very straightforward and to the point, with very little filter, whereas southerners like to ignore altercations and pretend somebody didn't just push them on the Undergound. That could never be me.
- In Manchester, dinner is lunch, and in London, dinner is tea. (In Manchester, tea is your evening meal.) Got it?

It wasn't until I moved to London that I really began to understand the differences between northerners and southerners. I didn't even realise we *were* that different until people insisted on telling me twenty-four-fucking-seven. It started off a bit funny, and, as I'm sure you can tell by now, I do have a good sense of humour. Taking the piss out of myself is one of my favourite things to do, and it's the very reason I'm writing this book (drink), so I'm very thick-skinned in that regard. However, when I was faced with middle-class white guys generalising the north as being 'rough', it did get my back up. It wasn't coming from a place of humour; these were genuinely their bigoted thoughts and beliefs. I remember once I was cooking pasta in our halls kitchen, and one of my flatmates came in. He was a Tory and wore Ralph Lauren, but also looked like he needed a jet-wash from head to toe. You know those posh kids that enjoy looking scruffy? They will wear white Vans that are absolutely filthy and covered in holes because they think it's gritty. It's their trademark. He was one of *them*. Anyway, there I was, minding my own business. I filled up a glass with water from the tap and he goes, 'I bet it's weird drinking tap water. You can't do that up north, can you?'

Excuse ME?

I was literally snatched. How *dare* he sit there and question OUR crisp, fresh, freezing, soft, quite frankly delicious tap water, when I'm here drinking your cloudy, dusty, crusty, bitty stuff? I literally laughed my head off. I don't even think I responded fully to what he said, because I was in such shock. He was literally an engineering student as well. Little did I know this was just the first of many such comments that I would go on to receive during my time at university. I must acknowledge my privilege in this situation: there are worse types of prejudice out there, and I am aware of that, but it was just a shock to see how people genuinely had these ideas about different parts of the country they were completely unfamiliar with. It's worrying.

SHOPPING LIST

Here's a list of cheap, cheerful and not-that-nutritious meals I enjoyed at uni:

- tuna pasta
- pasta
- pasta with pesto
- pasta with tomatoes
- cheesy pasta
- pasta with butter

Essentially, the key ingredients were pasta and whatever random shite you could find in the cupboards or fridge.

I also learned that doing your food shopping is so annoying. I never knew what to buy, and I couldn't stand how expensive shit was. I totally understand now why my mum didn't let me add Jaffa cakes to the trolley willy-nilly.

It's been a while since my last poem; I do apologise. Here's 'Avocado':

'Please place the item in the bagging area.'

I reluctantly throw down my £2.49 apricots.

'Fuck me, that's a lot,'

I say under my breath

as I start to scan the rest.

Tropicana Pineapple Juice, pressed,

a bag of Asda's Finest Salad,

boneless chicken breast,

Dairy Milk sharing bar

(*Pffffftt* 'sharing'),

tomato pasta sauce, six jars.

I spot some Haribo, reduced to a quid;

they were in a little pot, with a cute little lid.

So I bought five.

Finally I scan my £4 bottle of red

that will no doubt give me a sore head.

'Please wait while we approve this item.'

A supermarket woman strolls over.

'ID, please.'

I take my purse out with ease,

'There you are.'

'Excuse me, but that's your Nando's card.'

Bollocks. That was embarrassing.

I frantically search my bag.

'One sec, it's in here somewhere.'

The lady sighs, as she continues to stare.

'Look, I'm twenty. You've gotta believe me.'

'Without your ID, I can't sell you the wine, I'm afraid.'

And I just think, *Don't be a jobsworth, you'll still get paid*.

She confiscates the red,

so I swap it for a loaf of Warburtons bread.

It's not the same,

which is a massive shame.

Fuming, I smash the

'Finish & pay.'

That's a fuckin' lot to spend on a Tuesday.

£27.89.

And I didn't even get my bottle of £4 wine.

I hope this section about uni hasn't made you think that I had my shit together there, because I bloody didn't. I cried my eyes out after three days and strongly considered coming home. Within the first few weeks, I got tonsillitis, a chest infection, a sickness bug, and the worst case of thrush I've ever known. I once ate cereal with a fork because all of my spoons had disappeared from the kitchen, and I ate pasta with chopsticks for the same reason. But I am pleased to tell you I didn't become one of those students who displayed their empty alcohol bottles in their kitchen windows. Please don't be that person.

Musical interlude no. 9: 2015

Iconic songs from 2015:

'Sugar' – Maroon 5

'Bad Blood' – Taylor Swift feat. Kendrick Lamar

'Hotline Bling' – Drake

'What Do You Mean?' – Justin Bieber
'Hello' – Adele
'Elastic Heart' – Sia feat. The Weeknd and Diplo
'7/11' – Beyoncé
'One Last Time' – Ariana Grande
'Tuesday' – iLoveMakonnen feat. Drake
'Where Are Ü Now' – Skrillex and Diplo feat. Justin Bieber
'All Eyes On You' – Meek Mill feat. Nicki Minaj and Chris Brown

Much to my surprise, I was enjoying my course – and I was literally working my arse off. You know what was so gutting, though? I put 110 per cent into my first year at uni. I spent hours on my course work; I went above and beyond with my essays and my performances. I even cancelled a holiday because it clashed with a rehearsal. All that, only to find out that your first year equates to zero per cent of your overall grade. Yes, you read that right. *Zero*. I don't know why I didn't know that until I finished, but I was fuming. I wanted my £9,000 back. As I'm writing this, my best friend Gemma just said, 'You let it out, honey. Put it in the book.' Our favourite quote from *Mean Girls*.

MARCH (PART TWO)

Let's check in regarding me and March. We had been in our relationship for almost three years by this point; this was obviously the longest I'd ever been with someone, and it was going so well. I still loved her just as much as I did the first time I saw her. She had helped me settle nicely into London, and she was not only my girlfriend but also my bestest friend. I felt so held, supported and loved by her, which was so beautiful. We were changing each other for the better: I taught her about politics and how the Tories are evil and Labour are OK; she taught me about the importance of skincare and using expensive creams. March was a qualified beauty therapist, FYI, and a bloody good one at that. That's why 2016 was my

175

sexiest era, according to my photo album and Instagram page. My eyebrows were to die for, I never had a moustache, my nails were always gelled, my skin was popping off and my fanny was constantly waxed – all for free. March was so funny; she'd always say, 'You get a lot out of this relationship; think how much money you'd spend on all that I do for you. What do I get?' I used to say, 'I make you laugh, and money can't buy that.' Which was true. When I wasn't getting my arsehole waxed, me and March loved going out on dates. We were always out partying, dining or drinking.

THE MALE GAZE [GAGS]

This was obviously my first official 'out' relationship. So, I was discovering at first hand the amount of unwanted attention a 'fem-presenting' couple receive. We couldn't even walk down the street holding hands without receiving a look, a comment or even a grab. Yes, you read that right – a *grab*. I always assumed the issues we'd face would be homophobic comments; I didn't know that the issue would be with almost the opposite. Fetishisation. This basically means we are seen as objects who are simply putting on a show for the enjoyment of those watching (usually straight men). This reduces us to things that are wanted for consumption by privileged groups. Live, laugh and, yep, you guessed it . . . love ✌️. When I voiced these concerns to certain people, or talked back to the people abusing us, I would be faced with responses such as:

'You should take it as a compliment.'

'I don't blame them; you're both gorgeous.'

'Well, if you're out-and-out snogging, what do you expect?'

'Men will be men.'

'That's because you're like a wet dream, you two.'

'If you two are really lezzas, prove it.'

'One night with me, and I'd turn you straight.'

No, I'm not joking. People would literally say that. Until you're on the receiving end of that kind of abuse, you have no idea the weight that it holds. March and I were constantly on edge, not knowing what comment was coming next, or who was going to stare at us for holding hands. Kissing was out of the question. We would often get all dressed up and excited for a night out with our friends, enjoying ourselves, and then some heterosexual pervert would come on to one of us. We'd tell him we're gay and not interested, but then rather than backing off, he'd try harder. March would cry, I'd shout, and then we'd end up going home, because our night had been well and truly ruined. One time, after we told a guy to fuck off, he grabbed my arse, in front of March, simply because 'he could'. I would often tell March to calm down because these men could be genuine psychos and do anything to us if we tried to fight them. Which is even more sad. It got so bad that we stopped going out because of it. We couldn't face the harassment any more.

These harmful views are born from social media and pornography and music – all of which push the stereotype that lesbians exist to satisfy the male gaze, nothing more. Don't get me wrong, I love Drake's music, but some of the lyrics in 'Girls Want Girls' are very problematic. He's pretending to relate to lesbian sexuality in order to try and get with a woman who is clearly disinterested in him. Much like most of the men I have had the displeasure of encountering. So men, if you happen to be reading this, do better. Don't encourage your mates to try and 'pull' a lesbian. Being a lesbian means we categorically don't like men – your behaviour towards us is just further supporting why we don't. So, disrespectfully, *fuck* off.

This poem is a little different; it's written from both my perspective and the perspective of a man we encountered by the South Bank in London. I actually wrote it for my first assessment during the first year of uni. It is based on a true story. This is 'City Lights'.

We were strolling by the South Bank, taking in the scenery. It was one of those picture-perfect moments that I'm going to look back on and smile. For a while we watched as the reflections of the city lights shined bright, guiding us on an unknown journey through this – what seemed to be – pretty perfect night. I glanced down, to see the love of my life's hand squeezing mine. The other was kept occupied by a cup of red wine. As we walked, we laughed, and we laughed, and we talked and then we kissed. I felt this overwhelming gratefulness and I wasn't even pissed! Not yet, anyway. She smiled and I caught a glimpse of those beautiful eyes. They're so honest. She could never disguise her thoughts; never conceal the way she feels. That's one of the reasons why I love her.

It's your average Saturday night, just finished work and it's time to lurk the streets of London for a while. I walk past some very attractive females, I smile. They don't smile back. But I don't care, I'm hungry for them, I'm looking at them like a snack. At first, I thought they were fit mates . . . but I'm unsure, so I sit and wait. I've got the nerve to sit and observe, to watch them both like a hawk. They're holding each other the same way a man would hold his bird . . . I don't speak a word. I don't need to. I've got a front row seat of fantasy girl-on-girl action. I'm feeling something much stronger than attraction.

'Do you wanna go halves on a pork barm?' I asked while I tugged on her arm. Her eyes said she didn't fancy it, I said, 'Please, babe, you only have to have a bit.' She gave me the eyes, so I kissed her forehead. She gave in. My playful moaning and groaning was sharply disturbed by a man stood gaping on the kerb.

They're not your stereotypical fat dykes, that I really don't like. They're top quality. Sexy blonde and a slutty brunette . . . I wonder how quick I could get them wet . . . I feel as though I've seen them in something before, I can't remember the title. Although there wasn't just two of them, there was four. A woman just can't do what I can. I remembered the name of the video: 'Slutty lesbian whores gaggin' for a man.' That was them, I'm sure of it. Fuck it, right . . . 'Excuse me darlings, where you off to tonight?'

I felt the blood draining from my face. Happiness disappeared. My head soon became an empty space. The lump clogged my throat. I couldn't breathe. Clammy hands. My legs started to tremble as we continue to assemble down this cold concrete. I see him preying on us like fresh meat from the corner of my eye that he wants so desperately to eat. Her hand abruptly slipped out of mine, as if embarrassed. Public shame painted all over our faces. We shouldn't have held hands. I dropped the wine on the floor and I instantly wished we never left our front door. I wanted to disappear. Like magic. This feeling has been absent for a while, well, three weeks, to be precise. Which is pretty long for us. Her hands went from warm to ice. She felt how I felt. I absently winked at her and forced a smile, assuring her we'd be back home in a while. I once again found myself imagining that I was a man. Would this bloke still mouth off, like he can? No. He wouldn't. But to be born with breasts is to be oppressed, it means you'll never be the best, that's what they tell us anyway.

They're playing hard to get. Fulfilling my fantasy, I continue to imagine them explicitly. I like it. My imagination is running, sprinting wild, just like a child, I can't help myself. 'Come on girls, it's only a bit of fun.' I don't know why they're acting so uptight . . . two girls like this is any real man's dream come true, right? How dare they come out in public places, snogging each other's faces, and expect me not to stare? Kissing and touching each other . . . it's fuckin' unfair. I want a go. The sexy blonde one looks like she's crying, and the slutty brunette is trying to comfort her. They're walking – practically running – away, but I want them to stay so we can have a play, you know, a cheeky three-way. I know that girls love attention. It's like dangling a bit of meat in front of a lion's nose, my mind is undressing them from their heads to their toes. They want to tease us. I just can't help myself. 'I'd love to see you two on all fours.' Did they just tell me to fuck off? Ungrateful fucking whores.

'Just calm down, let's go.' She attempted to relax me; she could see me in my eyes I was about to blow. My overpowering red rage was postponed as I saw the tears in those beautifully honest eyes, about to overflow. My heart pounded in my chest. His eyes glaze, mouth wide open, saliva dripping. It's the male gaze, not even a blink. Like an animal at the zoo when it's feeding time. They don't stop to

think about the damage that's inflicted. They just can't help themselves, totally hypnotised by their sick thoughts, addicted to this Pornhub perception, made purely to give them an erection. It's not fucking real. We headed back, the night coming to an abrupt end. Hands in our pockets so nobody suspects she's my girlfriend. On edge, trying to avoid unwanted attention. We didn't mention a word to one another the whole way home. In my head, I was just waiting, anticipating, shaking at the thought of another comment. Anxious. My hands were exhausted and lonely, they're not used to being on their own. My fingers, once held and loved, were cold to the bone. I stared at the reflections of the London city lights: still, despite everything, they were shining so vivid and bright. But all of my optimism was stolen by the unforgiving night.

Fuckin' deep, right? And it's about to get a whole lot deeper. But before that:

Musical interlude no. 10: 2016

Iconic songs from 2016:

'Sorry' – Justin Bieber
'One Dance' – Drake
'7 Years' – Lukas Graham
'Pillowtalk' – Zayn
'Hotline Bling' – Drake
'Cold Water' – Major Lazer feat. Justin Bieber
'Let Me Love You' – DJ Snake feat. Justin Bieber
'Starboy' – The Weeknd
'See You Again' – Wiz Khalifa feat. Charlie Puth

I know what you're thinking: *What a great year for Justin Bieber.* Who, while we're on the subject, does make some absolute bangers. I just don't like him very much as a person, I don't think. I mean, I obviously don't know him, but he seems a bit cocky and full of himself. Justin, I can imagine you *will* be reading this, so no offence, but that *is* the vibe you give off. If you wanna change my mind, you know where I'm at.

All of those songs remind me of a holiday we went on to Portugal to visit my mum. It was one of the best holidays of my life. Me, Matthew, March and Luke hired two scooters to get about on. They only did a maximum speed of 30 miles per hour, so when we'd rev up hill, it was, quite frankly, embarrassing. Matthew let Luke drive one of the scooters on the road; he was twelve and could drive it better than I could. March also crashed ours into a wall and nearly broke her ankle; I lost my flip-flop. It was hilarious. It's bittersweet when I recall memories like that one, because I know I'll never ever have it again. Not like that.

TWENTY-ONE

The year 2017 was the year of my twenty-first birthday party. It was also the year that Trump became the forty-fifth President of the United States – gross – and the year of the Manchester Arena bombings. Which was incredibly hard-hitting, not only for Mancunians but everyone around the world. It was also the last year that everything was 'normal' for me.

I know what you're thinking: *So now you were twenty-one, did you have your shit together?* Absolutely fucking not. Not even close. Isn't it funny when you're a kid and you're convinced that by the age of twenty, you're going to be a fully fledged, functioning adult who does adult things like owning a house? Lmfao. My twenty-first was one of the best nights of my whole life. We had it at Stacey's gaff (obviously), and Mum hired these sumo suits for us to wrestle in the garden. We played drinking games, we danced, and we had such a laugh. March refused to wrestle with me because the suits were smelly and 'unhygienic'; she could be a bit anal and boring like that. My dad even said to me, 'WHY SO BORING?' I had to shush him. So

I wrestled with Luke instead. Everyone had gone to bed and me, Stacey and Luke stayed up until about 3am singing Beyoncé's 'Drunk in Love'. It's one of my most precious memories.

Gem was there too, which I loved. Gem is my bestest friend in the entire world – we've been bezzies since we were in reception and she is truly one of a kind, a real *gem*. She often says stuff that blows my mind. I like to call them Gems of the Day.

For example: 'When I'm doing a pregnancy test, I just wee into the toilet bowl and dip the test in there; same thing, isn't it?'

And: 'The world is 70 per cent water, so basically fish are like plants.'

I once told her she was like Nigella because she had cooked something nice, and her response was, 'Don't you mean Nelson Mandela?'

No Gemma, no I don't.

Musical interlude no. 11: 2017

Iconic songs from 2017:

'24K Magic' – Bruno Mars

'Wild Thoughts' – DJ Khaled feat. Rihanna and Bryson Tiller

'Black Beatles' – Rae Sremmurd

'Passionfruit' – Drake

'Bodak Yellow' – Cardi B

'1-800-273-8255' – Juanes and Logic feat. Alessia Cara and Khalid

'Look What You Made Me Do' – Taylor Swift

'Young, Dumb & Broke' – Khalid

'I Don't Wanna Live Forever' – Zayn and Taylor Swift

'Issues' – Julia Michaels

Grief

I'm going to delve into grief now. Yippee. Trigger warning: this section is explicit and heavy. A huge part of myself and my life is grief. It hasn't always been, obviously. I was introduced to grief during March 2018. Prior to this, I always used to think about how lucky I was to have all of my family still with me. My nanny was ninety-six at the time, and I couldn't believe she was still with us. I always dreaded the day that she'd go, because she was the glue that held our family together and we all loved her very much. At the same time, I was accepting of the fact that, one day, she would have to die, as much as I didn't want her to; I knew that that's just how life works. You get really old, and then you die. You live a long life, and then you die.

I never, in my deepest, darkest nightmares, imagined that I would lose Luke.

My fourteen-year-old nephew; Matthew's nephew. My best friend. A child. My sister's son. My mum's grandson. My niece's brother. Even writing this gives me chills because I cannot comprehend it, still. It goes against the natural way of life. It's wrong. It's backwards, it's sick – and it's my reality, one that I am still learning how to cope with. I will be learning for the rest of my life.

I remember every single tiny detail from that weekend. Some things I'll share and others I won't, because I can't bear to even think about them.

16 MARCH 2018

March and I were going to Center Parcs for the weekend with our mates. I was so excited, because I'd never been and had always wanted to go. I considered it a proper posh place, like the Tory version of Haven Holidays. (Which, while we're on the subject, absolutely went off. Tony the Tiger, I'm talking to you.) I remember being in the car on the way there; I think it was a two-hour journey. We were listening to all of our favourite songs, talking about all the cool stuff we were going to do. We arrived late and put the fire on in our cabin, and I drank Malibu and pineapple, and we played countless games of Cards Against Humanity with our friends. I spent the entire night laughing. It was a late night, and we had to be up early to go and do some activities. I went to bed a little pissed but very happy.

17 MARCH 2018

We woke up proper early and went to a climbing place; it was a bit like Go Ape. I remember it was absolutely freezing and had started snowing, so it was not a good idea at all, but of course, we did it, nevertheless. I remember my hands being so cold I couldn't even move them, so I'm surprised we didn't fall off. March bought me a pair of gloves, but they were shite and didn't help. I think she spent £6 on them.

After we'd tortured ourselves with Go Ape, we went to the Center Parcs waterpark – I was SO excited. I absolutely love waterparks, and this one looked so fun. I put all of my belongings in my locker, and off we went. There was this slide that went half outside in the snow, and it sent you proper flying. I convinced March and our mate Bethan to keep coming on it with me because it was so funny. Eventually, they got bored and went on something else, but I stayed on it by myself, 'cause I was enjoying it so much. I remember having a moment of tranquillity: despite being thrown the fuck around on this slide with a bunch of children, I felt so happy and at peace.

After a few hours at the waterpark, everyone wanted to go and I didn't. I was practically crying to March, begging to stay for another twenty minutes because I was having so much fun. She said no, so I got in a massive mood and reluctantly followed her to the changing rooms. I'm not used to not getting my own way, and to be honest, I don't like it.

I got all of my stuff out of the locker and checked my phone. I had eight missed calls from my mum and a text telling me to ring her ASAP.

I just want to sit in this moment with you for a minute. This moment before I called my mum back was the last time I felt whole. As soon as that phone call finished, a part of me died. My entire world was pulled from underneath me. It blows my mind that your life can change in a split second. I was just having the time of my life at a waterpark with my girlfriend and my friends, and I had no clue what news I'd be coming out to. And that absolutely terrifies me.

I remember the changing room door was to my right. I was standing on the left and March was getting changed to my right. My socks got wet from the floor, which made me furious. I called Mum back and asked if she was OK. I apologised and said I'd been at a waterpark. Her tone was different; there was something in her voice that I'd never heard before. She told me that Luke was in hospital and they'd been told he wasn't going to make it. He'd taken something with his friends, and he'd had a bad reaction.

I responded, 'What are you talking about? Why would you lie?'

She assured me she wasn't lying. 'They don't think he's going to make it.'

'Who doesn't think he's going to make it?' I remember saying over and over again. 'Don't lie to me. Why are you lying to me? That isn't true.'

Something took over my body and I collapsed on the floor. I remember the feel and the smell of it. Chlorine. I put my head into my hands and started to pull my hair, and I threw the phone to the other side of the room. I was hyperventilating; I couldn't catch my breath. March picked up the phone and spoke to my mum. She started to cry. I was in hysterics and denial. It didn't make sense. March picked me up off the floor and explained to me that we would go back. We'd go to the hospital now. I was in a complete daze as we left the changing rooms. March told our friends, and I didn't even look at them. I think I just looked ahead. We walked back to our room to get our stuff, and all of sudden, I snapped out of it.

I was convinced Mum was obviously being dramatic, so I started to laugh. I explained to March that we didn't need to go anywhere, he would be fine. He was probably being dramatic himself! March didn't look convinced by what I was saying, but obviously wanted to take my lead on what we should do. So, I got in the shower and started washing my hair. I was whistling. Now I can recognise that's because I was in complete shock; I couldn't accept what I'd just been told, so if I pretended it wasn't real, everything would be OK.

When I got out of the shower, I had a missed called from Alex, my brother-in-law. I called him back and it altered my state, again. I started to panic and hyperventilate once more, insisting to March that we leave right now. I was told that Luke was at Alder Hay hospital in Liverpool; we were currently in Woburn. That's over a three-hour drive.

It was snowing, so heavily. We ran to the carpark to try and find the car. I couldn't even see clearly because of the snow, and we had forgotten where we'd parked. Then my brother called me. I answered, and he was in absolute hysterics. I have never heard him cry in my life. He told me I needed to get to the hospital ASAP, as Luke was in cardiac arrest. I was beside myself. I couldn't breathe properly. I was screaming, 'Where is the fucking car?' I was shouting at people walking past, asking them where the fuck the car was. It took us ten minutes to find it; we were both in a state. March didn't even catch her breath and calm down before she started driving. We finally set off, and March was doing 100 miles per hour on the motorway in the snow. I'm surprised we didn't have an accident, but neither of us was even thinking of that.

That car journey felt like the longest of my life. It was complete hell. I was so desperate to get to the hospital quickly, and I couldn't get there any faster. I knew I'd be in the car for at least three hours. I rocked back and forth in my seat in silence the whole time. I remember we stopped for petrol and I called my nanna. She told me it was going to be OK, and I felt like maybe it was. I had calmed down a little bit during the journey, and I'd managed to convince myself everything would be fine once I got there. I was mouthing, 'He's OK. He's OK. He's gonna be OK,' while rocking back and forth for the duration of the journey. March was driving so recklessly to get us there quickly. I was texting Mum, telling her I was on my way, and that I would let her know how he was doing. Mum was obviously in Portugal, which was extremely difficult for her; she had no way to get there quickly.

We eventually arrived at the hospital, and Matthew was outside having a cig. He looked different; I'd never seen him look like that before. We went inside, and I remember it being massive. There were these swirly stairs going up the first floor, where we had to go. I went into the waiting room to see my sister and Alex. Stacey had a sense of calmness about her. She, like the rest of us, was in complete denial. It was very much, 'God, what's he like?' and 'He's going to be grounded forever after this.' She asked if I wanted to see him. Of course I did.

That was when I lost all of my hope. The second I walked into that room, I just knew. I knew. I saw all these machines, and I heard all these beeps, and I saw his precious face and his little body and I just knew. March had to leave the room, and I just sat there with him. I held his hand and I begged him to wake up. I remember the feel of his hand in mine. If I close my eyes, I can see how he'd cut his nails and I can remember the soft wave in his perfect hair. The smell of his aftershave on his neck. I was looking at him, and all I could see was my precious baby nephew. A cheeky smile, big blue eyes. A heart of gold. Lying in front of me, lifeless and cold.

It was a nightmare.

I was living in a nightmare.

The machine was keeping him alive, essentially. I was watching his heart rate on the monitor, and I was praying in my head that it would pick up. It didn't. It just kept going down and down.

There are details from this time that I can't write about. I can't bring myself to *think* about them, let alone write them down.

After around four or five hours at the hospital, we were all sitting in the room with him when the doctor came in and said something that I will never forget, that I will never be able to unhear. 'I'm so sorry, but he is dying and there is nothing more we can do.'

When you watch films and they play white noise when someone

receives news like that, it's true. My ears stopped hearing, my nose stopped smelling, my eyes stopping seeing. It's like my entire self was paralysed with this reality. I remember having such a strong physical reaction. My toes curled so hard in my trainers that I bruised them. I clenched my jaw so tightly that it locked. I ripped balls of my hair out into my hands, and I scratched my neck until it bled. None of that hurt. I was completely numb and couldn't feel anything physically. I could have broken my own arm and I wouldn't have felt it.

I watched my sister's eyes when the doctor said that to her. It was a pain so severe I wouldn't wish it upon my worst enemy. I watched her heart break with my own eyes. I saw a sadness in her at that moment that has never left. I heard cries that night like nothing I'd ever heard before. They were more like howls. The sound of true heartbreak and agony.

You never in your life imagine such a thing would happen to you or your family. You watch stuff on TV and say things like, 'God, I can't even imagine it.' I didn't have to imagine it, because it was literally happening.

We spent a few more hours with Luke. I kissed him on his head and I remember the feeling on my lips. One of my tears dropped into his hair. I couldn't believe this was real. Earlier that day, I had been at a waterpark having a nice time, and now our entire lives had been ruined. I had to call my mum and tell her they were turning off the machines. It broke my heart even more to have to tell her that. The sadness in her voice has never left me. I literally can't comprehend that what I'm writing is the truth. It still doesn't feel real, and it still hurts so fucking deeply. It's the worst pain in the entire world.

Leaving the hospital was bizarre. It was around 3am and it was snowing heavily. March drove us to my nanna's; I was in a trance. Nanna opened the door and asked, 'How is he?'

I had to tell her that he didn't make it. This was also extremely difficult. My nanna was howling. I was completely broken. I didn't know what to do with myself. I managed to fall asleep on the sofa for a few hours, and the morning hit me twice as hard because I realised it wasn't just a nightmare. It was my reality and it wasn't about to get easier.

THIS SECTION MIGHT HAVE BEEN INCREDIBLY
DIFFICULT FOR YOU, TOO/ HERE'S A BLANK PAGE
TO WRITE DOWN ANY THOUGHTS OR EMOTIONS IT
MIGHT HAVE BROUGHT UP. I GOT YOU.

This one is called 'Hospitals'.

Buildings that touch the sky
Daunting doors
and walls of beige
Nurses working tirelessly for minimum wage
The floors are all the same
Tears of joy and tears of pain
A last kiss goodbye
A new baby name
An infant carrier
to a walking frame
Will he make it?
It's a waiting game.
The place where life and death come hand in hand
Some expected, most unplanned
The smell sticks in your nose
on your hands and all over your clothes
Sanitiser and a cold shepherd's pie
You gaze out of the window into the sky
as the world continues to pass you by
despite the one you love about to die

It's always the same chairs
masked in a blue squeaky leather
You sink deep into its walls
trying to get your shit together
I watched you take your first breath in a hospital
And I watched you take your last breath, in a hospital
As a newborn baby started to breathe
me and my loved ones, started to grieve.

STAGES

I could continue to tell you about that week, that month, that year. The three years after that. The tears I've shed. The screams I've let out. The punches I've thrown into my pillow. All you need to know is a part of me stayed with Luke that night, and I never got her back.

And I started a journey, one called grief. I didn't choose to be on this journey, and if I had a choice, I'd do anything in this universe to avoid it, but time machines don't exist. So this is my life now. With this enormous fucking hole in the middle of it. I didn't know how to navigate from one day to the next. I was completely lost and completely broken. I still am broken, but a little less lost.

I'm not a medical professional nor am I an expert in dealing with grief. Aside from being devilishly good-looking and funny, I'm just a regular person who is battling grief. If you're reading this and wanting to be prepared for grief, don't bother. Nobody and nothing can prepare you for that feeling. What you do need to know is that it's not linear. Everybody's experience of grief is completely different; this is only mine, and I can only speak my truth from my reality.

Generally speaking, there are five stages of grief:

Denial

This is born from the feelings of shock and numbness. It's the body's temporary way of dealing with a rush of overwhelming emotion. It's like a defence mechanism: we pretend it isn't happening. This is completely normal, and I was in a state of denial for months, especially the first month, before Luke's funeral. The only way I could function was by imagining that it hadn't happened, despite knowing that it had. My body was telling me that it might not be real. This was just so I could make it from day to day.

Anger

Once reality starts to set in, you're face to face with the pain of your loss. The feeling of helplessness can lead to frustration and anger, which you will often direct towards other people and/or life in general. I remember being out and about for the first time after it happened; I think I was in big Tesco, getting some photo frames for the funeral, and I was absolutely livid at everyone around me for just living their lives. As if my family and I hadn't just experienced hell, as if we weren't broken; there were people buying ham and getting on with their lives. It's enough to make you want to hit them. I know that might sound dramatic, but it's true. I would also think about all of the people before Luke who had taken something with their friends and been fine, and all the people after him who would do the same and be fine, and I would wish that they had died instead. I just felt like nobody around me deserved happiness. The world deserved to just stop because my world had.

It's also normal to feel angry at the person who has left you. Luke had zero idea this was going to happen, and it wasn't his fault, but you can naturally feel anger towards the person who is gone. You want to say, 'Why did you do that?', and there is nowhere to direct those emotions.

Bargaining

This is when you start to dwell on what you could have done to prevent the loss of that person. It's always 'if only' or 'what if'. Again, it's completely normal. You will torture yourself with these thoughts. It makes me sick to think that while Luke was lying in hospital, I was on a waterslide with my friends, having a nice time. I always think back to my first night at Center Parcs drinking Malibu and pineapple and playing Cards Against Humanity – that was the night Luke fell ill. I should have rung him and seen what he was up to, or I should have texted him. If I had, maybe it would have altered his actions that night. I could have done something and I just didn't. This obviously isn't the case. I couldn't have changed what happened, but it's a normal stage to go through.

Depression

As life continues, the sadness sets in and you begin to understand the loss and the effect it's going to have on your life. I'm four years on, and I'm still at this stage; I'm not sure you ever come out of it. I've been on anti-depressants since it happened, and I don't want to know how I'd feel without them. The grief I experienced was very violent and traumatic; this will have a long-term effect on me.

Acceptance
I'm not there yet, and I'm not sure I ever will be.

QUESTIONS ABOUT GRIEF
I think we can agree that this section has been hell. Hard to read, even harder to write, but hey, you must know by now how much I rely on my Google searches – so I'll be your personal search engine for grief now. Off we go . . .

Can you only grieve over the death of a person?
No. There are many different types of grief. The death of a pet. The loss of a relationship. Changes in a relationship. Alterations in your way of life. The death of a person is only one kind of grief. When this first happened to me, I remember feeling really angry when I discovered that people can grieve over their pets. On reflection, I don't feel this way any more, and I myself have grieved over the loss of an animal. As I'm sure you know, it's absolutely devastating. For some people, it can be more devastating than losing a person, depending on your relationship with that animal. But at the time in my grief, I was angry with the world, and in my eyes, nobody's grief came close to mine. This is also a very common response.

How long should I grieve for?
I don't believe there is a 'normal' amount of time to spend grieving. Your process is individual to you and it depends on a number of factors, such as the type of loss. For example, if you lose somebody very suddenly, you are likely to grieve for longer.

Is grief just an emotion?

I don't believe so. I think it can trigger a lot of physical responses, too, such as dizziness, palpitations, fatigue, headaches, hyperventilation, nausea, tightness of chest and weight loss.

Do I need professional help?

In some cases, grief never goes away, and it doesn't always get easier to handle. You may not be able to accept the loss; this is something doctors apparently call 'complicated grief'. If you're struggling with any feelings of overwhelming grief, just book an appointment with your GP, especially if you're having trouble sticking to your normal routine and/or are thinking about ending your own life.

I've learned that while you're in deep emotional pain, it can be easy to try and numb it with alcohol, food or even work. Just be careful, as these are all temporary escapes that won't make you heal faster or feel better in the long run. Having said that (and I don't know how good this advice is, but this is my book, so fuck it), do whatever you can to get yourself through that initial period of grief. My family and I stayed up until around 3–4am most nights in the month before Luke's funeral, drinking, smoking and having a laugh. Which might sound bizarre, because we were absolutely broken, but it was the only thing we could do to get us through it. We kept each other above water, and we did what we had to do. Never, ever feel guilty for doing what you need to do to get yourself through, whatever it is.

After consulting a medical professional, therapy is always a good place to start. I do have some therapy horror stories that will make you laugh; I'll share some of those later. Never with Niamh; she's always been amazing. I just tried some other therapists while I was in London, and safe to say, they didn't help. But once you find that therapist you connect with, someone you trust, who you feel understands you, it's a nice release to discuss your grief in a safe environment.

WHAT NOT TO SAY

If you're lucky enough to have never experienced grief, allow me to tell you the things to *not* say to someone who is grieving.

'It'll get easier'

I understand this statement has pure intentions. However, it's quite frankly absurd and disrespectful to say this to somebody who has lost someone close to them. You cannot guarantee that things will eventually 'get easier'. Stacey, Matthew and I absolutely fucking hate it when people say this. It just isn't true and it's hurtful. Don't say it.

'I felt like that when my dog died'

Do not compare your grief with anyone else's. You might be doing it as a way to try and comfort them, but people can take great offence to hearing things like this. No type of grief is comparable to another. And you losing your cat doesn't compare to my sister losing her son, in my eyes.

'You're so strong'

I know this comes from a place of love, and a wish to assure the grieving person that they're doing a good job of carrying on, but sometimes you just don't want to hear it. It can belittle your emotions and make you feel guilty if others think that you're doing 'really well', or that you're 'strong', because that's the opposite of how you feel.

'Aw, don't cry'

Never, ever tell somebody what to do in that regard, nor how to feel. Never say anything like, 'You should start getting out of the house.' Again, I know this comes from a place of love and care, but it is never received in that way. You have absolutely no idea what that person is battling with, and it isn't your place to mess with that.

Sometimes I'll be amongst a sea of people and feel alone,
so, I gaze into the distance, wishing I was at home.
I unlock my phone
and open my camera roll.
I should have known.
I always do this.
I sit and stare at your perfect face, reminisce.
A fleeting moment of bliss.
Before I lock and put away,
I'll always stroke your cheek and give you a kiss.

COLLAPSE

Some people will absolutely collapse from grief; others use it to fuel them. Some people do both of those things. I'm one of those people. I have my days where I collapse, where the waves are too strong and they pull me under the water. On other days, the waves are gentle, and I go with the tide. I'm trying to accept that I'll always be in the sea of grief. Sometimes I'll ride the waves, other times I won't, and that's just my life now.

I made the conscious decision to make Luke the reason that I live: the reason that I achieve, the reason that I'm kind, the reason that I'm here. Because that's all I can do. I'd be lying if I said that I haven't thought about ending my own life because of the pain this is causing me every day, and sometimes it's really hard to ignore those feelings, but I know that ultimately, my family need me and I need them. So, for me, Luke is the reason that I carry on.

I don't have a title for this next poem. It's a bit of a spin off from '381', explaining the pain that is grief.

It's easier to just go
But that'll be the hole even more hollow
I'd be out of my pain, no more going insane

GRIEF

No more playing this game
Because I don't see the sunshine, only the rain
I don't hear anything, only your name
And I'm tryna be strong
Tryna prove my head wrong
I can get through this, here is where I belong
Until the noise becomes too much
Until the days are unbearable that I don't feel your touch
I read somewhere that
Grief is just love with nowhere to go
How do you live with that? Tell me because I don't fuckin' know
Give me the answers, because I'm too fuckin' low
There's a hole in my heart, it's fuckin' hollow

All I do is stare at your photo
How will I actually get through this? I don't know
Is this all a bad dream?
I can take back every tear, every scream
I'll open my eyes and there you'll lie
I'd be able to touch you, not stare at the sky
Not a feeling that just passes me by
Not a heartbreak that makes me cry
Not a pain that makes me wanna die
No more questions, no more asking why
No living without you, I'd take back my goodbye
I'd tell you I love you, and await your reply
You'd say it back, and I'd let out a sigh

You know when something is so real
But at the same time you almost can't feel
Like you're trying to stand but you can barely just kneel
So much time passes, but you've not even started to heal
The feelings you're trying to conceal

Are coming to the surface, ready for reveal
In life, there's so many solutions you can just throw
So many answers that people just know
But with grief, it's on the surface and there's nothing below
I've never felt the word 'nothing' so strongly before
But now it pains me to my very core
Because nothing is the answer to grief
There's no solution, no matter your belief
There's no fix, nothing to provide relief
Not even for a brief moment
After this is spoken
My heart still remains broken
My arms still remain open
My mind still remains hoping
The fear of nothing is still growing
Like you're aware of what's happening but the feeling is truly maddening
I'm stuck in between feeling too little and feeling too much
I'm in between coping and dying without your touch
I'm trying to keep my head above water
I'm taking my own advice, not forgetting what I taught her
I'm trying to be there for my family,
To be a good sister, auntie, daughter
But sometimes the pain of nothing is truly overpowering
I lose all of my senses, it starts devouring any ounce of hope I clung on to
I'm just trying to make it through
And it's impossible when all I want is you

I just can't comprehend it
This feeling inside, man I just wanna end it
You get your love ready to go and you send it
I read the book that you recommended
I wish I could say it helped, but there's no more pretending
Deeper into this reality I am descending

A deeper pain is just pending
This can't be my life, I didn't intend it
I'd do anything, my back I'd bend it
My hand I'd lend it

Grief is a journey and not a good one
Too much pain, you decide that you're done
You accept that this emotion has won
You let your arms go and you drop that ton
And in doing so pull the trigger on that gun
Because this is a feeling that you simply can't outrun

'SHIT, INNIT?'

So, this is the new me, I guess. Riddled with grief, trying to find my feet in the world again. Nothing felt important to me after Luke. It was less than two months until my final degree performance, which was worth 80 per cent of my overall mark. I was absolutely convinced I wouldn't be able to do it. I didn't have the strength nor the desire to even see anybody, never mind go and create a performance for uni. I had a meeting with my head of department, in which I totally broke down. Prior to this, I'd had a bit of a crush on her. You know what I said earlier: strong, intelligent, powerful women *do* something to me. It's a gay thing. Although now, in her office, I was literally snotting all over the gaff, ugly-crying, and rightly so. I'd blown any chance of her reciprocating that crush. Gotta laugh, eh?

I decided to stick it out; I didn't want to take a year's break and come back into a new class with people I didn't know and start the process all over again. I somehow mustered up the strength to complete my degree. It wasn't easy; I didn't want to do it. Obviously, I loved writing and creating and performing, but I was completely traumatised, heartbroken and ill – more so than I was letting on to my lecturers and friends. I couldn't be doing with the whole 'Oh my god, I'm so sorry' malarky. I didn't want to be wrapped in cotton wool. It was a waste of breath, because it didn't make me feel better, it just annoyed me – much like everything and everyone else at that point.

My university referred me to the mental health team, who later referred me for counselling. I use the word 'counselling' lightly. I went into a room with this lady, and I had to explain what had happened, which I couldn't physically do, because I was crying too much. I eventually wrote it down on a piece of paper, and her response was, 'OK, and I can imagine that's been hard for you.'

. . . You can *imagine*? No, It's been an absolute joy!

Then she proceeded to talk shite to me. As soon as I mustered up the ability to actually speak, she started to *yawn*. Yes, she yawned. I was fully crying my eyes out, breaking down, and she *yawned*. She even made the little 'ah' noise at the end of it. She didn't even try to be discreet. It was so fucking funny, because I was so shocked that I stopped crying and just stared at her in disbelief. I wish there had been somebody else in the room for me to give *that* look to. I eventually got referred for some more counselling, which unfortunately wasn't much better. *This* lady just repeated every single fucking thing I said back to me in a very patronising voice. Example:

ME

I just can't cope with this pain any more.

HER

OK, so what I hear is that you can't cope with this pain any more?

Yep. That's what I said. Don't get me wrong, I wasn't expecting miracles, and realistically I knew there was nothing this woman could do or say to make me feel any better, but I didn't anticipate it making me feel *worse*. I remember on another occasion, I had opened up a bit to her, and was having a deep conversation. She checked her watch *six* times as we were approaching the final ten minutes.

Sometimes she'd say to me, 'What do you think you should do?', and it's like, I obviously don't fucking know, otherwise I wouldn't be here. Another time, I told her I wanted to kill myself, and she suggested that I 'take a nice warm bath'. I thought to myself, *If I get in that bath, love, I am not getting out.* Live, laugh, love.

Another thing that really fucked me off was mindfulness. I still, to this day, couldn't tell you what mindfulness is. Let me consult my good friend, Google:

> Mindfulness means maintaining a moment-by-moment awareness of our thoughts, feelings, bodily sensations, and surrounding environment, through a gentle, nurturing lens.

I know what you're thinking: *WTF?* Right? It's basically some sort of meditation practice whereby you focus on being intensely aware of what you're feeling and sensing in that moment. I understand it's supposed to relieve anxiety and allow you to become more present. And I get it, I do. I'd even done those breathing exercises at college and found them somewhat helpful. However, how am I, a hyperactive girly with the shortest attention span, in the grips of an agonising grief, supposed to get anything from being intensely aware of what I'm feeling? When I try and *stop* thinking about something that's stressing me out, it's literally impossible; I end up thinking about it more. So if I attempt mindfulness, it just results in me thinking *more* about the things that are stressing me out – as well as focusing on the fucking car alarm I can hear outside. It's stress upon stress. Bit too artsy-fartsy.

Here are the six so-called principles of mindfulness, and why they don't resonate with me:

> *Non-judgement; being an impartial witness to your own experience* – This is just funny, because I would literally give myself the ick in that situation.
> *Patience* – I have never lacked anything more.

Open mindedness – OK, this I can't really argue with. I am open-minded. But one out of six just isn't enough, is it?

Trust – I can't trust my own feelings a lot of the time because they change constantly. I can't keep up with myself.

Acceptance – We know from past experiences that I have issues with this . . .

Letting go – Absolutely impossible. I can't let go of anything, ever.

You might be reading this and completely disagree; if that's the case, I am truly happy for you. I wish I could achieve that level of calmness. Maybe one day.

Niamh and I laugh about this now. Niamh knows me so well that she would never tell me to have a bath if I was feeling quite literally suicidey. She's good at listening, and always gives me the best comfort when solutions aren't possible. That's something I like to live by: comfort or solutions. If someone is upset and you can't fix the problem, just *comfort* them. If someone is open to suggestions that might help, provide them. Simple.

I hope my therapy stories haven't discouraged you from trying it. Like I said, Niamh is an actual angel, and I don't think I would have made it this far without her. Some therapists you'll like and some you will actively hate, but when you find the right one, it is so worth it. If you're not really ready to talk to someone yet, that's also fine: Dairy Milk, a cat and a weighted blanket could suffice for the time being.

GRADUATION

Yeah, you're right: 2018 had already been a horrible – and horribly long – year, and I'm sad to tell you that this part of the book is still not over. After my bout of shite therapy at uni, I managed to complete my final project, and I graduated with an overall first-class degree. This was a big moment for me: being not only the first person in my family to go to university, but graduating with a top mark, felt really nice. I mean, nobody has *ever* asked me about my degree mark since, but I am proud, nevertheless. Mum and

Dad came down to London for my graduation. It was cute to have them there together. I stole my hat (sorry not sorry). I needed something to take home and show my lot in Manchester, and I'm not being funny, but that's the least university owed me. A stinky graduation hat full of bobbles, reeking of debt and freshers' flu.

Once uni was over, I somehow found myself feeling the same as I had when I was doing my shitty call-centre job. Like, I'd worked my arse off for three years and now it was over, and I *still* wasn't a famous Hollywood superstar? (*King Julien's voice* HOW LONG IS THIS GOING TO TAKE?) One thing I learned once I left university was that they absolutely do not prepare you for life in the real world. Universities like to boast about being 'a vital stepping stone into the world around us'. I can confirm that this is bullshit. Maybe if you've completed a degree in nursing, for example, then sure! That is a vital part of becoming a nurse, and you absolutely can't be one without the right education. Acting, however, is a different story, and I have learned that the hard way.

What I find universal in most educational systems is that they do not teach you basic life skills. There's no lessons on how to generally survive as an adult in this cruel world, and this lack of guidance leads to various mental and physical health issues. Here are some things the education system did not teach me that I have had to figure out for myself:

- What a mortgage is and how it works.
- Why I have to pay tax.
- How to pay tax.
- How long to cook chicken for in the oven.
- How to save money.
- What a credit card is and how it works.
- Why houses are so expensive.
- The fact that, if you die, your student loan gets axed.
- That you shouldn't put a kiss at the end of every professional email.
- Self-defence.
- How to make a fire if you're stranded.

- How lesbians have sex.
- Why you should never put a tin of beans in the microwave.
- Why we can't just print more money.
- That Maggie Thatcher was a cunt.

Here are some useless things education *did* teach me, which I have never personally needed to know in my adult life:

- Pythagoras' theorem.
- How to say 'Please can I take off my blazer?' in French.
- The difference between an acid and an alkaline.
- How to throw a javelin.
- How to make a small wooden box.
- That I'm good at the bleep test.
- How to dissect a frog.
- How to play the recorder.
- Why my English teacher thought the curtains were blue in a poem versus why I thought they were blue.
- How to put a condom on a banana.

LOST

I really felt alone and lost. I'd dedicated three years of my life to a subject that I adored, and now it felt like I was back at square one, with some added debt and a few more friends – oh, and a portion of grief. During my last year of uni before I left, I had a job at my accommodation as a 'halls ambassador'. This involved being a student mentor and monitoring student behaviour within the halls of residence. It was as jarring and boring as it sounds. I basically had to shut down parties and grass on people for smoking weed. In return, I got to live in my accommodation rent-free, which I have to say was worth it. After what happened with Luke, I absolutely could not be fucked to do that job any more, so I used to just switch off my work phone and/or ignore any call-outs, until eventually I left and moved in with March and her family. I loved that so much. Not only was I spending most of my time with my girlfriend, I was enjoying eating Waitrose chicken and fresh tiger bread, and drinking coffee from a posh machine. All jokes aside, March's family very much treated me like their own daughter. I felt so loved, looked after and cared for at her house. Her mum washed and ironed all of my clothes, and always cooked the nicest dinners. Her dad gave the best cuddles, her sister felt like my own, and her little brother reminded me of Luke so much. It was a good place for me.

I ended up getting a job in a bar and food hall in Croydon called Boxpark; it was alright, actually. The hours were proper long and I sometimes didn't finish until 3am, but I needed money for my own things, and March used to pick me up most nights, which was very kind of her. I found it hard starting a new job with people I didn't know. Previously, I'd usually enjoyed making new friends, but this time I didn't want to meet anyone new because I was grieving, and I didn't want to explain that part of my life to anybody. Equally, I didn't want to just ignore it. I was a shell of a person, and it wound me up that these new people didn't know what I had been through prior to this job.

Anyhow, while I was slaving away cutting lemons and pulling pints (badly, I might add), my life continued to get worse. Only a few months after what happened to Luke, my sister was diagnosed with cancer. You couldn't write it. She, of course, didn't care; she didn't feel her life had any value anymore anyway. The people around her obviously didn't feel that way. I'd never wanted to take a pain away from somebody more. I think it was stage two, which wasn't amazing, but also wasn't the worst. She eventually had a mastectomy, and she was OK. It was just horrible to see her going through this physical pain on top of the worst emotional pain imaginable.

In general, people say bad things happen in threes, so I was just waiting for the next thing. And so it came. This seems like an appropriate time to insert a very fitting quote.

I was held at gunpoint with Junior and Princess in South Africa, my mum being told she was dying, my German shepherd got killed on my driveway, my horse got killed outside my house on the dual carriageway, Harvey had a kidnap threat and then I caught my husband cheating.

– Katie Price (2019)

This is giving very me-in-2018 vibes.

So, after Stacey's cancer, her house got broken into. This obviously doesn't come close to what had already happened that year, but what made it unbearable was that the burglar went into Luke's bedroom, which had been kept completely untouched, exactly the way he'd left it. And then this bastard went rummaging through his stuff and moved everything. This was heartbreak upon heartbreak, as we'd never get the room back exactly the way he left it. Ever.

I posted a tweet with a security-camera video of the man who'd robbed Stacey's house. It went viral, and he was arrested. Obviously, we were happy about that, but the damage was done and could not be reversed.

Shortly after this, my nanny died. It was old age. The natural way. I remember feeling awful, because I couldn't cry. I think it didn't touch the sides compared to what I'd experienced earlier that year. I felt like my nanny's death didn't get the reaction from me, Stacey and Matthew that it would have had if we hadn't experienced our loss. Stacey couldn't even bear to go to her funeral. I hadn't seen Nanny that often since I'd moved away, so I had been unable to notice how poorly she was getting, but she had started to lose it a bit up there, so she never really understood what had happened to Luke. We knew this was a good thing, because that knowledge alone would have killed her. I remember feeling a bit peaceful at the thought of Nanny joining Luke, wherever he was. I knew he'd be happy to see her.

I have always believed in life after death, FYI, but even more so after everything that happened that year. I felt things for the first time in my life after Luke. I saw feathers and robins, and I had dreams and visions. I talked to him out loud most nights, and I'd either laugh or cry. Or both. I'd say things like, 'I bet you're listening to me going on, thinking, *Shut the fuck up, Soph*,' and then I'd piss myself laughing. I think I probably would have been sectioned, had anyone been watching me. Sometimes lights would flicker, or walls would bang. I was never, ever scared, because I'd convince myself it was Luke letting me know he was there. It got me through a lot of shit, really. Stacey and I went to see a few mediums, which absolutely blew me away. I don't care who believes in them and who doesn't; I know for a *fact* they're real. Some mediums have told me things nobody in the world knows apart from me. The information wasn't on social media, and I had given them zero information – not even my name – before I got there.

When I tell people I believe in life after death and that I believe in fortunes and mediums, they will often say, 'Load of shit, that,' and that's fine if that's what you believe, but don't push that narrative on to everyone else. A medium told me once that Luke loved my speech at his funeral so much, and then proceeded to describe Luke's bedroom in immense detail. Nobody knew I had made a speech apart from the people who were there, and nobody had seen his bedroom apart from family. There were no photos of it anywhere. Ever since Luke left us, I have been certain that there is something after we pass. I sometimes feel him around; it's really strange and I can't really describe it. It's more of a feeling. In a strange way, I did find comfort in knowing Luke was still around, that he could see what was going on and that he was there in his own way, but it also made it harder, because I just wanted to see him, talk to him and hold him.

At around this time, I was entering my new phase of grief: depression. I booked an appointment at the doctor's and basically told them that I didn't want to be alive any more. I was so sad with grief, I couldn't even bring myself to get out of bed most days. I would sleep until I had to go to work, and that was literally it. Every night, I'd go to sleep praying that I wouldn't wake up in the mornings; it was a painful and vicious cycle. The doctor prescribed me 30mg of Citalopram and sent me on my way. I remember feeling weak that I'd given in to antidepressants. I wanted to be able to handle these feelings on my own, but it just became too much. I was worried for my own mental health. (It's worth noting that it is absolutely not weak to take antidepressants; I think doctors hand them out willy-nilly these days, but if they work for you – do it.)

I was desperately searching for a new job, something within the industry that might help me want to live a little bit more. Eventually, I found one. It was a front-of-house job at the Lyceum Theatre in London's West End, home of Disney's *The Lion King*. I had no idea what to expect, but I was excited to just be in a theatre, surrounded by like-minded individuals. The only issue was, it was in central London, and I was living in Surrey with March. I had to walk, then get a bus, and then a tube. It took a really long time, but I was willing to travel if it might have improved my will to continue living.

After my first few shifts, I loved it. I was still unhappy, but I was enjoying the job. I made some lovely friends, and I was watching *The Lion King* what felt like forty times a week. The only issue was that my hours completely clashed with March's. She worked nine-to-five, and I worked six-to-eleven. By the time I'd travelled home, everyone was in bed, asleep. I began to feel very lonely, but I didn't want to compromise the job, as it was the first time since uni that I'd felt as though I was getting closer to achieving something. Even though I was serving Sauvignon to mostly rude, middle-class arseholes, I was in a theatre. Which would do for now.

JULY (PART FOUR)

In the middle of all this, I received a message request on Facebook. It was from July. I should probably mention that July had tried to contact me numerous times over the years, and I had always ignored her. I had told March about July, and how in love with her I had been, so naturally March didn't want me to have any contact with her. Deep down, I knew that was for the best, as I imagined it would be very easy to become attached to July again. And so, we'd not spoken for around five years. That doesn't mean I hadn't thought about her, or checked her social media, because I sure as hell did.

In her message, July told me how sorry she was to hear about Luke. July had had sleepovers with me and Luke back in the day, so she was another link to him, in a way. I told March about this, and I also told her I was going to reply this time. I had realised that life is too short, and I no longer wanted to ignore July for the sake of March, because if anything happened to her (God forbid), I would live in regret and I didn't ever want to do that. So I replied, and we arranged to meet for a coffee in Manchester. I told March this was happening, and she wasn't happy, but I did it anyway. I wanted to and I felt like I had to.

I remember seeing July, standing waiting for me in the train station. It was the first time I had seen her in so long. My heart sank, and I felt a tiny bit of that feeling she always gave me. It felt like my entire body was on fire. My heart sank into my chest, and I felt hot and overwhelmed. It was under the surface, but very much there.

We went for a coffee and we spoke for hours. I told her everything that had happened since school. She apologised for the way she had treated me, and explained that she wished things had been different. I asked her if she was happy. She hesitated, and said yes. She was in a long-term relationship, much like mine. Eventually, I had to leave, and she walked me to the station. She got on to the train with me and gave me a hug and a kiss on the cheek. She also gave me a necklace. It was silver with a wishbone on it. It was all a bit like a fever dream. I was in love with March, I was hugely unhappy, and I'd just been given a necklace by the girl who broke my heart.

ENDINGS

March and I had just had our five-year anniversary, and I still loved her, so much, but I just couldn't shake this feeling of being unhappy. It was obviously because of everything that had happened. The antidepressants didn't seem to be working, and I continued on a downward spiral. March was the only thing left in my life that was good – so, naturally, I wanted to destroy that. I felt like I didn't deserve any happiness whatsoever. I had started to self-sabotage every aspect of my life that I was still enjoying. It was the only thing I could do.

I told March that I wanted to end our relationship. I told her I wasn't happy, that I wanted to kill myself, and that I wanted to be alone. This is devastating for me to write, because to think about how unhappy I felt, and how much I hurt March with that decision, makes me feel sick. She didn't deserve to have her heart broken by me. I just felt like I couldn't give her everything, because I was so sad. I needed to restart *everything*. I think maybe she was a reminder of what had happened, too. It was a catch-22 situation: I didn't want to lose her because she made me feel closer to Luke, because she had been there, but I also couldn't stay with her, because I felt trapped in it all.

I think ending a relationship when you're still in love with the person is absolutely agonising, but very brave. I had never been able to imagine I could live without March. Not only was she my girlfriend, she was my best friend and my life partner. And I had just thrown that all away, for practically no reason at all – because my gut told me it was the right thing to do. I was so numb, I hardly felt anything. I was alive, but I was lifeless. Losing March meant losing all of my security, my home, my second family. Everything. I had originally moved to London with the idea that I would be there with her forever; now I had completely shattered that. I packed some bits into a small suitcase and I went to stay with my friend, Holly, on her sofa. I think I stayed there for a month. That month was *one* of the hardest of my life.

Musical interlude no. 12: 2018

Songs that remind me of the worst year of my life ☺ :

'God's Plan' – Drake
'Nice For What' – Drake
'Feel It Still' – Portugal. The Man
'New Rules' – Dua Lipa
'SAD!' – XXXTentacion
'In My Blood' – Shawn Mendes
'Happier' – Marshmello feat. Bastille
'Say Something' – Justin Timberlake feat. Chris Stapleton
'Moonlight' – XXXTentacion
'Changes' – XXXTentacion
'IDGAF' – Dua Lipa

Yes, I do know how problematic XXX Tentacion is; I think that's testament to how sad I was. I was still listening to his music. Gross.

APRIL

Now that I didn't have March, I had truly lost any form of happiness. I was still enjoying my job, but that wasn't enough to make me feel happy. I had shed a load of weight, so much so that all of my clothes were hanging off me. I was drinking most nights, and I was behaving recklessly, not caring about the consequences of my actions – which was usually my style anyway, but if you combine that with feeling suicidal, it was not a good mix. This was also my first time ever being single (basically), which I couldn't even try and enjoy because of how sad I was. I didn't realise until I left March how bad I am on my own. I missed having someone to share things with and someone to provide comfort for me. I know what you're thinking: *Why on earth did you leave March, then?* I know. But I did, and there was no going back. I'd made my bed, so I had to lie in it.

You might be thinking, *OK, why don't you go back to July?* As far as I was aware, she was in a relationship, and she was happy. I wasn't in a place to disrupt that.

I eventually met someone new at work. For the sake of this book, I will call this person April. She was very fun, funny and kind. I didn't plan to like her in the way I did; it just happened very naturally. We were spending pretty much every day together at work, and she went from a friend, to a close friend, to a friend with benefits, to my girlfriend. Within a matter of months. This completely went against everything I had planned for myself. I wanted time alone to sit with my grief, time to rebuild myself and focus on work. It never does happen that way, does it? April was great, and she tried her best to support me in any way she could, especially with my grief – which was, of course, not easy. She couldn't make it go away.

I eventually moved off my friend's sofa and into my first flat. Alone. It was a room in a house share for £600 a month. Extortionate. It was shite, but it was the first time I'd gained any independence. I went to Ikea to kit myself out with some nice bedding and fairy lights; you know how it is.

I was still in touch with July here and there, but I wasn't really giving her the time of day, and I wasn't in a position to have my heart broken by her again. My head was all over the place, and I didn't think I'd make it from one day to the next. It was like, all of a sudden, my entire life had changed, again. I'd gone from spending every day with the same person in a familiar place to being in a different part of London on my own – and it was all my choice. Strange . . .

I remember one day going to meet March for lunch. I told her about me and April. She was upset, naturally, and so was I. We ended up drinking a bottle of wine. After March left, I bought another bottle from Sainsbury's and I went down to the Thames to drink it. I was absolutely pissed and so depressed. I took off my shoes and started walking down the steps into the water. I was fully prepared to go in. It was minus-one that day, and I was so drunk that I couldn't feel the cold. One of my friends from *The Lion King* ended up coming to get me. I don't remember much because of the alcohol, but I'm glad she did. She took me to work, as I was due to start my shift in thirty minutes. My lovely management team sat me down, gave me crisps and water, and let me sleep it off in the office for a bit, then sent me home. I didn't even get into trouble; I think they felt sorry for me and understood I was having a hard time. I also don't think they realised that I had been just about to end my life in the Thames . . . but hey, the ready-salted Yorkshire crisps *did* help the suicidal thoughts subside.

That was one of my lowest moments, and it was difficult to understand, because I was lower in February 2019 than I had been in March 2018. Now I can understand that it's because I was in shock at first; once reality starts to kick in, that's when you really start to feel it. For me, that happened an entire year later. I'd like to share a heartfelt quote with you that always helps me through my worst days.

Love a bitta lemon in the sweet.

That's what I used to think Jesy Nelson was singing.

SURVIVING

So, I was just about surviving in 2019. It was a rough start to the year, but I managed to pull myself through. I don't know how I did it, I just did – I think the thought of my family losing me as well was enough to keep me going.

I'll tell you what I did learn that year: how fucking shit, annoying and out of order being an independent adult is. I'd had a taste of that at uni, but really at uni you're just a child doing adult things. Now I was like a proper, *proper* adult. Like, I'm not being funny, but why the fuck is my electric bill so high? Why is ham so expensive? Why are there always clothes that need washing? Why is having to make tea every night so exhausting? Why do things go off so quickly?

I wasn't enjoying my independence and freedom. It's funny, because when you're younger, you're so desperate to grow up, and then when you're grown up, you want to revert back to being looked after. Unless that's just me . . .

I was a year into taking my antidepressants, and I was wondering if they were doing anything at all, given that I actually felt worse. This one is called 'Citalopram'.

I'm depressed.
Sometimes I want to kill myself.
Instead, I go on the Ikea website and order a floating shelf.
Gifts for me, to provide a temporary relief.
I like to call it:
'Retail – try not to kill yourself – therapy'.
Distract my mind to pass the time with online shopping:
ASOS, Amazon and Deliveroo, I'm overstocking.

Sometimes I can't get up
like I'm nailed to the bed, like I'm stuck
with a hundred-kilogram weight pressed hard into my chest.

I'm anxious and shaking, I'm stressed.
Before the day has even begun
whether it's raining or blazing sun
I stay under the covers.
I see everything in grey, there's a lack of colours
in a metaphorical sense, of course.
People will say: 'What's making you sad?'
And I don't know the source.
It's everything and nothing at the same time.
People say it's a long journey, it's a steep climb,
but I feel myself slipping.
I'm trying to hold on, I'm gripping.
The rope I'm holding is ripping.
I search for my inner strength.
No quitting.
The voice inside my head saying *Do it.*
I won't listen.
In my mind I scream and shout,
but through my mouth the words won't come out.
I don't know what to do with my pain
Worst thing is, there is nobody to blame.
So I just take another pill.
Yeah, you bet I will.

'The easiest and least painful ways to commit suicide.'
There's literally an online guide.
I'm not going to tell you if I've tried.
I know that's what I've implied,
but I want to do something memorable before I die.

I'm fighting through each day,
trying not to overthink.

214

I'm working hard to keep my head above the water,
trying my best not to sink.
When the water's getting deeper and I'm going under,
I remember I can't drown if I keep my feet on the ground
and try to keep calm
to prevent causing myself any harm.
I know that being brave is the only way to
save
myself.

After less than three months in my overpriced and lonely flat, I moved in with April. Yes, it was quick, but I wasn't adapting to life alone very well, and it felt like the right thing to do – the time we had been together wasn't an issue for either of us, we were just going with the flow, which was nice. We moved to Canada Water, and shared a lovely house with two of our friends. It was so, so lovely. It was the first time I'd lived with friends in that way, and I had so much fun. I started to feel slowly brighter as I got settled into my new home. We had a nice little garden, and a cat next door. It was nice to not be alone, which is ironic, as I'd thought that's what I wanted and needed. I soon discovered that was, in fact, *not* the case. I think I love the *idea* of being alone more than actually *being* alone. I am too attention-seeking to enjoy just my own company; who's going to laugh at me?

I was loving my time with April so much – she was everything someone could want in a relationship. Kind, giving, a great listener and communicator. But ever since losing Luke, I was still struggling to feel whole or happy. I'd had the same issue when I was with March, and I worried it would never go away. I spoke to April about these feelings a few times, but we decided to keep going and try to make things work. She was determined to help me through this.

Musical interlude no. 13: 2019

Iconic songs from 2019:

'Old Town Road' – Lil Nas X
'7 Rings' – Ariana Grande
'Shallow' – Lady Gaga and Bradley Cooper
'Sweet but Psycho' – Ava Max
'Breathin' – Ariana Grande
'How Do You Sleep?' – Sam Smith
'Bad Guy' – Billie Eilish
'Someone You Loved' – Lewis Capaldi

Doomsday

The year you've all been waiting for: 2020. The year of the global pandemic, or according to Twitter, the global . . .

PANDEMIC WORD SEARCH

M	P	N	P	A	E	A	B	O	P	T	R	G	O	P
A	L	A	A	N	T	E	A	R	A	F	D	I	N	A
T	A	U	N	A	R	P	C	A	N	D	O	P	C	N
C	R	A	D	D	A	I	O	M	O	E	N	A	O	O
P	A	V	E	U	E	I	D	I	R	K	A	N	R	A
A	S	E	M	I	K	M	N	P	A	N	D	E	H	I
N	O	P	O	A	V	P	I	A	M	J	E	T	A	A
I	P	U	N	U	N	W	E	M	A	O	O	T	I	N
N	A	R	I	M	P	U	K	U	O	B	P	O	I	C
I	N	T	U	Q	U	A	N	D	R	O	A	N	L	O
S	E	X	M	Y	M	Z	N	Q	U	L	R	E	M	N
P	A	N	D	A	O	P	O	D	H	N	A	M	P	O
O	A	I	U	M	E	B	U	T	O	C	M	E	I	O
P	A	N	O	R	A	M	I	C	H	R	O	N	O	R
O	N	E	T	T	E	O	R	A	M	O	A	N	D	E

PANORAMA
PANDEMI MOORE
PANDORA
PANINI
PANORAMIC
PANDEMONIUM
PANETTONE

LOCKDOWN

Can you *literally* believe we lived through it? My book, the one I'm writing (you thought I'd forgotten? Ha! Drink!) might end up in some history section of a library one day when I'm long gone, not only because it's a great book, but because I, Soph Galustian, lived through a pandemic. So, if it's the year 3000 and you're floating around high school during your History lesson, using my book as a reference to how the year 2020 went down – welcome! I imagine not much has changed, apart from the fact we now live under water, according to the early 2000s pop-punk band, Busted. OK, I'll tell ya exactly how it was. This was the year my career started to change and progress, so strap in tight. This one is exciting.

I think the UK got wind of the virus in January 2020. I remember hearing about it on the news and on Twitter at around that time, and not really understanding what it meant. If anything, at this point it was a tiny bit exciting, because nothing like this had ever happened, and there was word that we'd be sent home from work because of it, which was thrilling, for obvious reasons. I quickly learned that it was far from exciting. By mid-January, COVID was an international concern and by 11 March it was a global pandemic and we were facing the prospect of a national lockdown. I'm not a scientist or a historian, nor am I going to try and be one, so I can only tell you what I got up to while the world was going to shite. I think, globally, we all hopped on a lot of the same trends. Allow me to refresh your memory.

Baking bread

Fuck me, did I bake a *lot* of bread. Mostly banana bread, which was very dry, and it only counted if you took a photo of it and posted it on your Instagram story.

Puzzles/painting

I've never really been a jigsaw kind of girl, but I thought I'd give it a go. It was alright, although a bit boring. The painting was fun for a while, until I fucked up and ending up punching a hole through my canvas and throwing it in the garden.

218

Zoom
This, my friends of the future, is a video-chat thing. We absolutely digged it during lockdown, and we still do. It's like being in a room with people without having to take your PJ bottoms off. Result.

TikTok
I am ashamed to admit that I did try and reject TikTok at first. I am a hardcore Vine girl, and I felt as though that's where my loyalties would always lie. However, it didn't take me long to jump on the trend, and when I tell you I'm obsessed, I am OBSESSED.

Tiger King
This was a very strange documentary about a man called Joe Exotic and his arch enemy Carole Baskin, who allegedly killed her husband. The show also involves tigers. It was a hot topic. *sings* 'Carole Baskin, killed her husband, whacked him/ Can't convince me that it didn't happen.'

Yoga with Adriene
Shout-out to my girl Adriene, who helped me start enjoying yoga. I know, who would have thought it? I would do fifteen minutes a day in the mornings, and it was kinda cute. I especially enjoyed her dog, Benji.

Googling 'what time is Boris on'
Everybody anxiously awaited Boris 'Bumbling' Johnson's announcements regarding the pandemic, which were always difficult to understand, and often left me more stressed and confused than before.

The Lyceum closed their doors and furloughed us pretty much straight away, which meant no working. No leaving the house, and one very hot summer of doing fuck all. I was grateful to have the girls and April at this point; we tried to make fun out of anything we could. A trip to big Tesco's was considered a luxury, and a walk to Decathlon to look at swimming caps was an even bigger one. We were only allowed one hour out of the house every day, which was for 'exercise', so I'd walk in a couple of circles around my local park and then head back home. It was ever so boring.

At the same time as our lives becoming so boring and repetitive, the virus was becoming more serious, and people were genuinely dying from it, which was heartbreaking, and filled everyone with even more fear than before. So we were bored, but we were also frightened.

381

So, it was time to create my own fun and find something I enjoyed doing – apart from wrecking paintings and getting impatient with jigsaws. Let's take it right to the top of this book: '381'. I did mention in the introduction that my poem '381' was the first one I ever posted. I had written it just before lockdown started, and I posted it on 28 April 2020. I'd had an OK following before this, of, I think, around 2,300 followers, but I never expected my first poem to go viral. The video of me reciting my poem was viewed over a million times, and shared by viral pages on Instagram, Facebook and Twitter. It even made its way into newspaper articles – no, not the *Da*ly Ma*l*. You might be wondering how it went viral. Did it happen by chance?

Did it fuck.

I literally sent my poems to as many people as I could on Instagram until I was blocked from messaging any more. I would send them to around 200–300 people a day. Who did I send them to, you may ask? The list of people would be as long as this book (drink) so here are a few of my favourites:

- Michelle Obama
- Snoop Dogg
- Kim Kardashian
- Lady Gaga
- Ariana Grande
- Phillip Schofield
- Ant & Dec

- Jade Thirwall
- Aitch
- Simon Cowell
- Charity Shop Sue
- Gwyneth Paltrow
- Molly Mae
- Peter Jones
- Dawn French
- Kehlani
- Kerry Katona
- Harry Styles
- Lindsay Lohan
- Stevie Nicks
- Daisy May Cooper
- Beyoncé
- Justin Bieber
- Joe Biden
- Matt Cardle
- Greta Thunberg
- Ruth Langsford
- Cardi B
- Jeff Bezos
- Alan Sugar
- Dwayne 'The Rock' Johnson
- Maxine Peake

I hope you enjoyed reading that list as much as I did writing it. What the fuck was going through my head when I sent my poem to Cardi B? I really did try and cover all bases. I have learned the hard way that unless you're rich or have family in the industry, it is incredibly difficult to be given the time of day, so I took matters into my own hands and harassed a load of A-list celebrities to watch my work. This was the thrust of my messages to them. (And if you're wondering, no, I didn't copy and paste the message.

I custom-wrote them for each individual; I felt like that may have given me a better chance. Besides, what if Michelle Obama discussed my work with Matt Cardle, and they compared the messages? They would know I'd been lazy and had copied and pasted. That was not a risk I was willing to take.)

> Hey Stevie! I am a huge fan of yours. I'm a writer from Manchester, and I wrote this poem about free school dinners. I'd be SO buzzin if you had a spare few minutes to watch and enjoy my work. Lots of love x

Don't laugh. Kidding, you can laugh, it is funny. I was gagging to be noticed, and I am pleased to tell you that hard work *does* pay off. Lady Gaga didn't reply, but the UK's comedy sensation actress and writer Daisy May Cooper did – equally as great, if you ask me. As more and more people were seeing my work, I began to slowly but surely grow my platform. I was getting out one poem a week, usually about current issues, so they felt fresh and relevant. Obviously, we were smack bang in the middle of a global panini, so . . . here we go:

> This pandemic has birthed more than one virus.
> People alone at home debating what their life's worth
> wanting nothing more than to disappear,
> convinced life would be better without them here.
> We're bombarded with COVID graphs,
> COVID this and COVID that,
> missing the biggest killer at hand
> but let me explain the real maths.
> 'Make space and wear your mask.'
> But wearing a mask is a real task.
> Now don't take this literally, I need you to think about it.
> Their mask is a smile, when deep down,
> they wanna quit.
> They're on the NHS waiting list.
> Eight months have passed,

they've had enough of having to exist.

Mental health is constantly put last.

They clench their fists in frustration,

the loneliness and the segregation

is nothing more than an abomination of how our leadership have

handled this situation.

The sense of loss is endless.

Loss of income, loss of routine and family time is suspended.

Not seeing a soul in seven months, I can't even comprehend it.

I've been in the place of wanting to end it

One in ten people expressed suicidal thoughts,

but it seems our interests lie within what's being bought.

Helping the economy stay alive, while real people are struggling to survive.

Now is the time to be kind.

If one person helped one person

the situation wouldn't continue to worsen.

Make people feel like they're worth it.

This won't last forever,

I promise the tunnel is lit.

You're not alone in this.

Don't suffer in silence.

You've got one life,

and believe me, it's priceless.

If you're a child of the future in the year 3000 and you're wondering what this one was about, I've got two words for you: Tory government. They absolutely fucked it. I mean, they always do in any situation, but Boris's 'handling' (if you can even call it that) of the pandemic was a fucking disgrace. I'm sure you're wondering, *How can I, too, write a poem about my government that doesn't give two fucks about me or anybody I love, and is more interested in making profits and following through with Brexit, which everyone knows was a huge mistake?* Well, let me tell you what *I* do.

Recipe for: The perfect poem

1. A large glass of red wine. (If you don't have red wine, any other alcoholic beverage of over 13 per cent will be sufficient to get us in the mood.)
2. Music. (Depending on the content I'm going for, I like to have sound to vibe to in the background. Sometimes I get distracted from writing and I look at myself in the mirror and admire how beautiful I am. Don't worry if this happens; it's completely normal and should subside after a few songs.)
3. A tablespoon full of depression and/or anxiety. (This one can help with the depth of your writing, especially when attempting the hard-hitting stuff.)
4. A dash of childhood trauma. (We all have it, and it makes for great storytelling.)
5. About 350ml of jokes. (What's a better way to navigate your way through words than with comedy? Provide some light comic relief for your reader so they let out a chuckle in between tears.)
6. A sprinkle of gay. (I don't know about you, but I can't do anything without it.)

DA*LY MA*L

So, that's how I did it. I found it easier to write about stuff that made me sad or angry, or both. This contrasted with my enjoyment of and passion (hate that word, soz) for comedy, but it was a great way to release and share my feelings on hot topics, which many others seemed to share. So that's how I spent 2020, cooped up in my very hot bedroom, writing about things that fucked me off.

You might have noticed earlier I mentioned the forbidden *Da*ly Ma*l*. I don't hate too many things in this world, but Christ, I have burning fire in my stomach for that waste of paper. It is vile, and if you read it, you're also part of the problem. After what happened to our Luke, lots of shit newspapers wrote articles about it. The information – if you can even call it that – that they shared was completely false, insensitive and hurtful. My sister even had journalists coming to the house days after it happened. How can you be so fucking disrespectful?

I'm not even going to carry on. Just read this. 'EXCLUSIVE':

Red-top tabloids spreading lies time after time,
so I'm gonna speak my mind in this rhyme.
Fake news should be a crime
and I'm about to tell ya why.
It's not just a paper but a construct that has so much influence on our society,
printing lies and causing anxiety,
hurting families and forming rivalry.
They employ a form of writing known as tabloid journalism,
aka fascism, racism and truth vandalism.
It's read by millions, as it supposedly understands and openly
articulates their concerns,
but in turn
it's falsity is spreading like a virus.
Everyone who wears a burka is apparently part of ISIS.
More or less everything causes cancer: 116 household items,
according to that paper.
It's one of their many tales.
Males can't do wrong and women need to pipe down.
OMG, she's had Botox! I can't see her frown!
Female celebrities that 'dare to bare' on the beach are subjected to
microscopic scrutiny of their physique.
Women who grow their body hair are nothing more than freaks.
These papers have the support of the majority of our politicians,
people in important positions
support the published superstitions.
It's nothing more than a book of lies
that accomplished middle-aged men
swear by.

They're immigrant-bashing, Muslim-smearing, woman-hating,
gay-baiting lazy writers.
They know what headline will attract the buyers.
Now let's get fuckin' real.
They're allowed to outright lie about people and situations,
causing complications within conversations.
They've no regard for human feelings, people are grieving and all they
care about is what people are reading.
It's personal to me because it affected my family,
two days into hell and they're reporting on our tragedy,
which, in my opinion, should be against the law; their number-one
source was Facebook – say no more.
The aim is to incite hatred in the comments;
some of what people say makes me want to vomit.
It's all nonsense.
Gammon-headed fucks with no conscience,
tied up in this false content.
People's private lives and struggles shouldn't be newsworthy.
These are real people and they're hurting, show some mercy.
I'm not even done.
Don't even get me started on Hillsborough and the *Sun*.
Posting vile hate back to back,
and all of a sudden it's 'What a shame about Caroline Flack',
when last week you were on the attack.
One of their slogans should be
'Putting profits before human values'.
Any petitions against their articles will lose.
They're distorting reputations and lives,
they're deliberately validating prejudice in their readers' eyes.
It's nothing less than clickbait culture,
the headline is the carcass and you are the vulture.
They act as Tory propaganda,
spreading Boris love and Corbyn slander.

Not to mention the demonisation of mental health,
Brexiteers, anything that wasn't man-made in Britain,
get it off our food shelf!
People in poverty are the constant butt of the joke, ah ha, it's so funny,
we're rich and they're broke.
'There are over 100 genders' 'Are our kids too woke?'
Front-page news: 'OMG – Meghan Markle spoke!'
And Kate's opposing treatment is a bit too frequent to be a mistake.
The readers respond with, 'Get over it, snowflake.'
They don't care for your opinion unless you're white and straight.
They've got the moral fibre of a piece of steak.
The way I feel towards them is beyond hate,
it's time to speak ya mind, it's never too late.
This isn't the way.
These papers are what's wrong with the UK.
There's no denying, so stop buying,
the truth on these pages is sparse,
their spelling and grammar is a farce,
I wouldn't even use their newspaper to wipe my fucking arse.

Mic DROP. That is one of my favourite ones to perform, I feel like Eminem in *8 Mile*, post Mom's spaghetti . . .

SKETCHES AND SCRIPTS

My poetry continued to help my platform grow, and I reached 10,000 followers on Instagram. I remember, years ago, a friend told me that if you have loads of followers on Instagram, it helps you get work. I didn't know how true that was – yet.

Once I grew more confident with my poems, I started posting little comedy sketches. Such as 'Things you hear too much of when you're a lesbian', or 'A middle-class dinner' (which was basically me taking the piss out of posh people, as they deserve). I received hundreds of messages from so many people from different walks of life. Some people messaged me sharing their stories of grief after losing brothers, mothers, sons. Other people told me that I'd inspired them to start writing themselves, and some people simply thanked me for putting into words how they were feeling. I don't have the words to describe how those messages made me feel – and still make me feel. I find it unbelievable, and also overwhelming, that people find comfort in what I'm doing, and that they feel comfortable enough to share their personal journeys with me. Some people have told me to keep going, no matter how tough it gets. To those people: thank you. Every single message I have received has touched me in one way or another. Especially Lee223Mac, who messaged me to say: 'Sexy tits need cumming on.' That one was beautiful.

I soon discovered that hard work really does pay off, as I received a message from a producer called Molly. She explained that she had come across my work after the wonderful Daisy May Cooper shared it (didn't want Beyoncé to share it anyways), and she asked if I'd like to have a 'general'. So, yes, I did immediately google 'what is a general'. She basically wanted a meeting with me, so she could introduce herself and I could introduce *my*self, and we could talk a bit about what we both do and maybe explore the possibility of working together in the future. This was the first door that opened for me, and I was beyond ecstatic. I had wanted an opportunity like this ever since I could remember. I told Molly about all of my ideas, goals and aspirations for the future, and she was the first person to give me the time of day and make me feel like what I wanted to create was attainable. And not only attainable, but *good*. Molly showed interest in everything I said. Don't get me wrong, I had always believed in myself, but it was so nice to have someone else believe in me for the first time. I sent over some scripts I'd written that were simply collecting dust on my laptop, and she *loved* them. She asked for my permission to send them to a lovely commissioner at the BBC called Emily. I obviously said, 'Thanks so much, but no thanks.'

JOKE.

I couldn't believe what I was being asked. I had never, in my wildest dreams, imagined that a producer or a commissioner would want to read my work. I didn't even really understand what a producer or a commissioner *was* before that moment. I remember getting off the call and crying my eyes out, because I was so overwhelmed and in shock that I had even got myself to this place.

At this time, I didn't have an agent. Don't get me wrong, I'd had them in the past, and by god, had I had some awful experiences with them. I actually paid to sign up with my first-ever agent. Rule number one: *never* pay to join an agency. They got me zero work and I was down £300.

Once, I went to meet another of my old agents in a very bougie members' club for a 'work chat'. As I've mentioned, my dad is Persian, which makes me half-Persian. Quick maths. This agent wanted me to have some new headshots done wearing a hijab, which I thought was wildly inappropriate. Armenia is not an Islamic country, to start with, and also, it would be so wrong and disrespectful towards Muslim culture for me to pose in a hijab purely for casting purposes. I told him about my aspirations of becoming a successful comedy performer and focusing on my northern roots, to which he responded: 'Nope – too many of them. You won't get anywhere.' Then he proceeded to tell me how my casting is 'Persian, hijab, Farsi speaking'. *I don't even speak Farsi.* He was trying to put me into a bracket that I simply didn't belong in.

It gets worse.

He then said, 'I will only put you up for what I think you're right for. For example, if a casting comes through for someone of a slim build, I won't be putting you up.'

My jaw honestly hit the floor. What was the actual need for that very strange and unwelcome comment? I wasn't sure if he was trying to hint that I needed to lose weight, or if he just lacked social skills. Either way, I was *out of there*.

So, I think it's fair to say I was sceptical about getting another agent – until Molly introduced me to Dawn. Dawn is my current agent, and she is, to put it plainly, *incredible*. She supports me in everything I want to achieve, and genuinely believes I can do it. So, fellow actors, if you happen to be reading this, never settle for less.

One thing led to another, and Emily loved the script. Lo and behold, Molly and I got commissioned to write the bloody thing for the BBC! That is how *Peck 'Eds* was born (I will tell you about that in a bit; hold your horses). When we got the news, I didn't have anything to celebrate with at home, and I was absolutely skint. But I did get this proper posh glass bottle of balsamic vinegar for Christmas from April's mum, so I opened it and took a swig in celebration. It was the best balsamic I'd ever tasted, to compliment the best news I'd ever received.

We were slowly approaching the end of 2020 and somehow, despite a global pandemic, it had been one of the best years of my life career-wise, and it felt like only the start. The progression in my career was rubbing off on my mental health, and I started to feel a little brighter about my future. The thought of being successful and being able to look after my family was my driving force. I was still writing as many poems as I could, and putting them out often in order to keep up people's interest in me and what I was up to.

I wrote this one that December. I was feeling really confused: I was so happy about where my work seemed to be heading, but also so sad that Luke wasn't here to experience any of that with me. One thing I'd noticed is a lot of people would say, 'Oh, have a lovely Christmas,' or 'You'll enjoy your Christmas now,' because of my good work news. Don't get me wrong, it was, of course, *so* exciting, but I should let you into a little secret of mine. I may as well, I've fucking told you everything else about me. I *hate* Christmas. I used to love it when I was a kid; it was my favourite. I loved being with my family and I loved getting gifts and all of that, but since Luke, I hated it. It feels wrong to enjoy a time that is supposed to be about family *without* my favourite member of my family, you know? No offence to the rest of my family that may be reading this – obviously, I love you all, but none of you will ever compare to Luke.

> For me, Christmas used to be my favourite time of year:
> filled with family, festivities, love and cheer,
> now if I'm honest, it fills me with fear,
> I can't celebrate when you're not here.

To others, that doesn't seem clear.

Why does Christmas make you shed a tear?

You sit around the table, with your roast and your crackers,

but it's not what's inside them, it's who you pull them with that matters.

It's the memories and the laughter

the late-night Baileys and the natters,

Nan having too much to drink, and feeling rough the morning after.

Of course, receiving presents is nice,

but please don't try and give me your advice

on how I should be happy, 'it's the season to be jolly' –

I don't care about tinsel, baubles or holly.

Some people love it and that's OK,

but for others, it's the worst kind of day.

It highlights that somebody is missing.

Every Christmas I find myself wishing

not for gifts, but for you to be living.

This love inside me is trapped, it can't be given.

The pain I feel is one in a billion.

So, I say

enjoy the time with the ones you love

while we think about the ones above.

If anything, remember them more on this day.

I miss him more than anything – I'd bring myself to say

for so long I felt bad for feeling sad on the 'best day of the year'.

You don't have to hold back your tears any more, my dear.

It's OK to be down, don't hide your frown,

let your tears build, drop and fall on the ground.

You're only human, after all; people handle grief in different ways,

big or small.

There's no right or wrong. We all fall.

For my darling, this Christmas

I can say now because I'm able,

there will always be a chair for you at our table.

Musical interlude no. 14: 2020

Iconic songs from 2020:

'Blinding Lights' – The Weeknd
'Watermelon Sugar' – Harry Styles
'Golden' – Harry Styles
'Adore You' – Harry Styles
'Everything I Wanted' – Billie Eilish
'Savage' – Megan Thee Stallion
'WAP' – Cardi B feat. Megan Thee Stallion
'Rain On Me' – Lady Gaga and Ariana Grande

BEGINNINGS

OK, so twenty-fucking-twenty-one? Where has the time gone? We were still smack bang in the middle of the pandemic, which seemed as though it would never end. One of the great things about this time was furlough and universal credit. I think I was claiming too much at the time, but at the end of the day, so what?

Here's a list of things I ordered off Amazon during 2021:

- Veet hair lightening cream
- bike phone holder
- yoga mat
- pornstar martini kit
- deep tanning oil
- notebook
- foot-peel socks
- outdoor hammock
- salt lamp
- after-sun lotion

- hand sanitiser
- 100 masks
- a paint-by-numbers kit
- a fan
- a corkscrew
- Feminax.

Honestly, that was the general vibe of the year. It was fucking red hot, and all I did was drink, sunbathe, write and have period pains. We did get to make my BBC Comedy Threesome, though: *Peck 'Eds*.

Peck 'Eds is a female-led, coming-of-age, out-and-out comedy about the testing moments of growing up as a young, working-class woman in South Manchester. It is also a celebration of what it truly means to grow up in this specific part of the country, based on lived experiences and real surroundings. We will follow the journey of Melissa and her group of BEST friends to get a taste of true council-estate life. From period troubles to first snogs, *Peck 'Eds* will blow the dust off these awkward memories, and bring feelings of nostalgia flooding back, along with an extra-large portion of cringe. Telling female, working-class stories is so integral to our society, and what better way to explore this than through comedy?

Peck 'Eds represents so many people from underprivileged backgrounds stumbling through high school. I can relate to the story I am telling, most of which will be based on real-life experiences, either my own or those of the people around me. There is so much stigma attached to being working class and from a council estate, especially within school. Programmes such as *Benefits Britain* brand places like Stockport with a low-class label. I want to reclaim and proudly own that label. I don't want to paint a glossy, idealistic image of council-estate life, as this would obviously be false. However, I want to create *Peck 'Eds* so people can laugh with us, not at us. This will reach a wide audience, as some will be able to relate to it, like a flashback of their youth, while others will learn from it, and hopefully gain a wider understanding of a female-led, working-class community through a comedic lens.

And that, folks, is a nice little overview! Basically, it's similar to this book, bitta funny shit that's happened in my life. It's still on BBC iPlayer, FYI, so give it a watch if ya want. No worries if not.

We filmed it in August, and it was one of the greatest moments of my life. Being on my first television set, surrounded by cast and crew that were all there because I wrote something. I had to keep taking myself off to the toilets to:

A) nervous poo
B) cry

I'd cry because I was so overwhelmed. I was literally living in a dream, and I was experiencing that impostor syndrome I'd had a small taste of back in my Stagecoach days. What is impostor syndrome, you may ask? According to the *Harvard Business Review*,

> Impostor syndrome is loosely defined as doubting your abilities and feeling like a fraud.

It's basically feeling like you do not belong somewhere. It can be a general low hum in the background, or it can manifest as extreme self-doubt and a fear of failure that is literally paralysing. I'd dreamed of this moment for so long, and even though I did believe in myself, I'd also sort of worried that it would never happen. But now here I was: I wasn't dreaming and it was happening and I wrote it for the BBC? W H A T? This is what I had wanted ever since I used to sit in my room as a kid, cold and hungry, and dream about being on TV and making people laugh. So impostor syndrome can *fuck off*. I wanted to soak up every single second, and I bloody well did.

Here are a couple of techniques I've found useful for battering impostor syndrome:

- Don't forget that you are not alone. According to our good friend Google, after publishing her eleventh book, Maya Angelou said: 'Uh oh, they're going to find out now. I've run a game on everybody.' Sis, same.
- Psych yourself up. Own your own accomplishments and remind yourself why you're worthy of being in that room. Write them down in a list or literally look at yourself in the mirror and say them aloud.

Once I'd told myself 'I'm the shit' in the mirror three times, it took us two days to film three short episodes. (Apparently, it's amazing that we pulled it off.) Before I knew it, I'd bagged another writing job with the BBC to join a writer's room for an upcoming comedy series. Again, this was an absolute dream, and I couldn't fathom that it was happening.

As I continued to progress within my career, my agent always reminded me to be present and enjoy exactly what I was doing in this moment. I have to work hard at that, because I am always thinking about what's next; I think that's partly for financial reasons, and partly because I am so hungry for this. I never want it to stop – it's what keeps me going and keeps me striving for more.

I continued to achieve things that I never thought possible. One of those things was being a guest on the award-winning podcast *The Guilty Feminist*, hosted by the wonderful Deborah Frances-White. It was a bit like a fever dream, because for so many years, I'd listened to that podcast in the bath, and I had always hoped I'd be a guest on it one day. We recorded it in front of a live audience at Soho Theatre, a place I had dreamed of performing in. I had to remind myself that I wasn't 'lucky'; I had worked my arse off for so many years to get to this place, and I truly deserved everything that was coming my way.

So, work was going well for the first time in my life; so much so that I had decided to quit my job at *The Lion King*, which was soon due to open up its doors to the public again after a very prolonged closure due to

COVID. I like to call that 'quitting my muggle job', which I believe is a dream for a lot of creatives. We normally have to work to live and then create to maintain happiness.

I have to be honest, I didn't have a lot of money. I think I was probably making less than I had when I was working front-of-house, but that didn't matter, because I was finally doing what I loved, and as long as I could pay my rent and eat – which I was just about managing – I was doing OK.

I'm sure you're thinking, *Soph, I know you by now. This is all too good to be true.* And you'd be absolutely right. Time to throw another spanner in the works. But before I do, have another poem. This one is called 'Dusty Van' and I performed it on *The Guilty Feminist* and during an online vigil alongside Sandi Toksvig and Jeremy Corbyn (cool, right?).

I explore the street, nervously.
My key rests between my fingers, purposefully.
My knuckles turn white as I clench so tight.
I consider ordering a taxi that I can't afford
to safely deliver me to my front door.
But then I panic, what if the driver likes me?
I just want to get home safely.
I hear footsteps behind me,
I clench my fist and grip the key
tighter,
ready to apply self-defence.
My legs start to shake; my shoulders are tense.
A woman minding her business overtakes me.
I let out a sigh of relief.
She innocently walks her dog,
she vanishes into the night as she starts to jog.
I desperately want her to return.
I want her to sense my concern
of being a woman
alone in this night.

It's snowing, but strangely, sweat forms on my forehead.
Why does walking home alone fill me with such dread?
Because some men have made us feel unsafe in society.
They've filled us with self-doubt and anxiety.
As they shout out of their dusty vans about
where they'd like to put their hands.
If you ignore them, you're ungrateful.
If you entertain them, you're shameful.
We're called a 'bitch' for being assertive,
and we're called 'cute' for being nervous.
And it'll still somehow be our fault
on the receiving end of this assault.
For a man to confirm his masculinity
we must highlight our societal given 'stupidity',
deprive ourselves of our strong femininity.
We're seen as heavenly if we still have our virginity.
We're only good for cooking and cleaning.
We must only speak when spoken to, no intervening.
Being a woman is mostly being misunderstood.
We're confused for weak, for no good.
We must not forget that we have a lower social stature than a man.
We cannot achieve half of what he can.
We're weak in the body and in the mind,
like he can see, and we are blind.
We've got no backbone, we're too kind,
and if we're strong, we're unrefined.
So, get back in your lane.
It's no place for a woman.
Life is a man's game.
We are not equal, and we are not the same.
If we're silent, then we're still the ones to blame.
'Maybe your skirt was too short?' he said.
'I mean . . . you could have said no?'

'You could have fought?'

'You must have led him on.'

'Once you came around, he'd already gone.'

'That's convenient. She's probably lying'.

'Attention-seeking. Fake crying.'

Even when we wear brightly coloured shoes

and we don't touch a sip of booze,

we're alert and sensible,

but men still choose

to murder us.

But still #notallmen, don't make a fuss,

and don't forget:

if you're scared, just flag down a bus.

We know it's safer to say nothing

and conform to your gender role.

To not be too ambitious and certainly don't have goals,

because these men hate progression.

They want us to drown amidst our oppression.

It's time for times to start changing.

This world can be ours for the taking.

Don't let them win,

don't give in.

We can't rewrite history, but we can create herstory.

Enough is enough of the patriarchy, let's introduce diversity

universally.

Daughter, auntie, niece, nanna and mother:

we're are united as one, we are the other.

We'll fight together, one another.

I know it's a lot to digest

thrown to the ground at a peaceful protest

for speaking your mind, you're under arrest,

it's for your own safety, it's for the best.

Talking of safety, I say this with my chest:

until we stop being murdered, we're never gonna rest,

because

no amount of violence

will have us silenced.

We are a force to be reckoned with.

Let's show what we can give.

One voice, one stance,

and it stands.

She has the world,

in the palm

of her pretty little

hands.

Deep, right? Fucking sick to my back teeth of being a woman, trying to survive in a patriarchal society . . . but, yes, hold your horses. I promised I'd tell you about my spanner in the works.

JULY (PART FIVE)

So, work was thriving, but something was still missing for me. I knew that not having Luke would always leave me hollow, and I was beginning to understand that this was just the new version of myself. However, what I was feeling was more than that.

I haven't spoken much about Niamh in these later pages, but you should know, we were still in regular contact, and she was still trying to help me heal my trauma from school (aka July). Niamh and I have been talking about me and July for the past eleven years. Throughout my relationships with July, March and April, I have never been able to close that door and move on.

I want you to know that things were good with me and April; I loved her, and I was happy with my life with her, but I often felt as though *I* wasn't complete. I just got sick of feeling this way for July, even after all this time. We weren't in regular contact, but we had been in touch here and there over the years, and the three of us (me, July and Niamh) eventually came to the conclusion that we should have a joint therapy session. Crazy, right? I told April that this is what I wanted to do, and explained that I felt like it may help me to heal my trauma. She was incredibly understanding and encouraging of this, despite feeling understandably upset and uncomfortable about it. Having said that, you know by now I'm the kind of person that would have done it regardless.

I came back home to Manchester for the session. I liked to come back when I could to stay with Stacey and have a bit of family time, although obviously COVID had made that difficult recently. I loved coming to spend time with my niece, Emily, who by this time was eleven, very cheeky and becoming a mini version of my sister. She reminded me of Luke in some ways. I always wonder what their relationship would have been like now. Anyways, I came back for a few days to perform poetry at a couple of gigs in Manchester, and arranged my therapy session for the last day of my trip.

I was hungover for the session, which wasn't ideal, but what can you do? I was trying to act like I was very calm about the situation, which I absolutely wasn't. I hadn't seen July in so long, and I was so scared about how it would make me feel – even more so after how I'd felt last time. I'd imagined scenarios of us bumping into one another, and what we'd each say, do, feel. Niamh knew what a big deal this was for me. Years of confusion over July's feelings, and years of pain over mine, were finally being addressed.

I saw her standing outside the office door as I approached, and there it was, that feeling again. My heart sped up, my palms started to sweat and my mouth trembled – still, after all this time. She smiled at me ,and it was as if I'd been transported back to 2010 (the only difference being I was now sexier, with better eyebrows and hair). We hugged, and she smelled the same and felt the same. It sort of felt like home, which was difficult to accept, given where I currently was in my life. We went inside and Niamh hugged me tightly, and then July and I sat down in chairs next to each other. I could hear my heart pounding in my ears. I was trying to predict what July wanted to say or get off her chest. I had spent so long thinking she didn't care about me at all, so I was preparing myself to hear that from her – but what I did hear was the complete opposite.

For the first time in my life, I heard her say the things I had longed for. She told me that she had thought about me every morning and every night since we left school. She regretted the way she had treated me and she wished things had been different. She loved me. She always had. She wished that we hadn't given a fuck about what people thought about us in school. That we'd not forced ourselves to be apart based on other people's opinions. She told me that she didn't see her future without me in it. The last time I'd seen her, she had addressed some things from school, but never like this.

As I'm sure you can imagine, my mind was absolutely gone. The words coming out of her mouth were words I had been waiting to hear for what felt like my entire life. I now finally got to tell her how *I'd* felt in school. How she'd absolutely ripped my heart from my chest, and how I had loved her so deeply. I wasn't angry at her any more; I understood her anxieties around being open in school. Even though we both regretted that now, ultimately, it's how things were at the time, and I don't think anything could have changed that. It's part of a societal progression that we are still fighting for.

It was like popping a high-pressure balloon for both of us, finally being in a safe space without judgement, where we could speak freely about our feelings for one another, both past and present. The session lasted two hours, and it felt like two minutes. I blinked and it was over, and all of a sudden it was time to go back to London, to my life, my partner, my friends. Spending those two hours talking to July had completely taken me back home, and the thought of going back to London to get on with things was very discomforting for me. I was flooded with emotion from the session, which I imagined would probably subside after a few days.

I wasn't ready to leave – two hours to discuss twelve years' worth of trauma just wasn't enough. July walked me to the station and we said goodbye, which felt so wrong and rushed. We hugged, and off I went – not knowing what my future looked like, not knowing if or when I'd see her again. All of a sudden, I was fourteen and broken again. I always listen to the music from 2010–11 because it's nostalgic and makes me feel a lot. So I popped on Rihanna's 'California King Bed', and off I went on the Avanti West Coast home.

I questioned my entire life after that session. Not just my feelings about July, but also being in London, wondering where home truly was. It unlocked a lot of hidden emotions that I hadn't confronted in a while, from missing home, to missing Luke, to questioning whether I belonged in London any more. You might be thinking, *You obviously felt that way all along, you just didn't know it*, and you might be right. Sometimes it can take certain people or situations or moments to bring things to the surface for you.

I walked through the door, and everything felt different. Suddenly, it didn't feel like home any more, which was so confusing, but I know before it always had. April greeted me warmly as she always did, and the guilt I felt completely consumed me. She could tell straight away something was off. We sat down and spoke for hours and hours about everything. Not just the session, but my feelings, anxieties and worries – and hers. April is an amazing listener, and always makes me feel heard. I brought up the fact that I'd never felt whole and that I didn't know how to cope with that any more. I knew that it was mainly because of Luke, but now I was questioning if it was also because of July, which I think I'd known on some level all along. After a long and painful conversation, April and I decided to end our relationship, and I was set on moving back to Manchester.

I didn't feel much at the time; I don't think I'd registered that my entire life was about to change, again – because of a decision I had made, again. We were together for nearly three years, and they were three happy years. April taught me so much, and I don't regret a second of the time I spent with her. I was learning, though, that sometimes you meet people, you spend time with them, and you each serve a purpose in each other's lives, and then you move on. I didn't know what my future in Manchester looked like, I didn't know where I'd live, I didn't know if I'd see July again, or if I'd still be able to work – everything was uncertain. But once again, in true me-style, I took a run and jump, and hoped that it would work out.

Musical interlude no. 15: 2021

Iconic songs from 2021:

'Easy On Me' – Adele
'Remember' – Becky Hill and David Guetta
'Ghost Town' – Benson Boone
'Cold Heart' – Elton John and Dua Lipa
'Montero (Call Me By Your Name)' – Lil Nas X
'Woman' – Doja Cat
'Peaches' – Justin Bieber feat. Giveon and Daniel Caesar
'Happier Than Ever' – Billie Eilish
'Up' – Cardi B
'Prisoner' – Miley Cyrus feat. Dua Lipa

HOME

So here we are: 2022. I moved home at the end of December 2021, and I moved in with my best friend Gemma, who is now a very put-together cute adult who has a whole-arse house to herself, so I've got a lovely little bedroom there, and living with her has been a dream. She washes my clothes, cooks my tea and vacuums my room – and, on the plus side, she makes me laugh. I think we used to talk about the idea of living together when we were kids.

I can't lie, it was tough at first. Adjusting to not being in London after seven years there was huge, and leaving my life behind to start afresh was hard at times, but I knew I had overcome worse in the past. I always keep that in my head: I lost the most important person in the world to me, and

I am still here, writing this book (drink), so everything else I can handle. I don't know if that's a toxic way to think, but it sure as hell gets me through – and what did I tell you before? Do *anything* you need to if it gets you from one day to the next.

I spent a fair few days in bed crying, and other days I spent laughing and feeling like I'd made the right decision. Going from living in central London to my small village was a huge adjustment, but ultimately it didn't take long for home to feel like home again. I soon discovered that home wasn't a place, it was a feeling brought on by people.

I know what you're gagging to know, so yes – July and I are now official. I CAN'T BELIEVE I GET TO WRITE THAT. Fuck. It became apparent that we had never stopped loving each other, and we owed it to ourselves and our history to give us a proper go, and so we did. And guys – wow. My life finally makes sense in so many ways. I'm not even going to hold back here, so get ready for very gay cringeyness. July is and always has been the absolute love of my life. I tried for so long to ignore that and block her out, to move on and pretend she didn't exist. I did that for literally years, but I can tell you, a day did not go by that she wasn't on my mind. Everything I did in my life made me think of her, even the most boring moments, and I have always wanted to share my successes and my failures with her. She was always there, at the forefront of my mind, and I would ask Niamh how the hell I could stop thinking about her – which was, of course, impossible.

As soon as I allowed myself to have her completely, I felt things I didn't even know possible. I feel on fire when I'm in her presence, and she feels the same when she's in mine. We are completely intertwined, and I have never known a love like it. We have spoken about *everything* from our past, and we often describe it as grieving; we are grieving for the time we spent apart, despite both spending that time with other people whom we loved and do not regret being with, by any means. All the same, it's difficult to acknowledge what we put ourselves through. When I find myself getting stuck in my head about this, I try to remember that July and I needed to go off and live our lives, make mistakes, make memories and find out who we truly are before coming back together.

According to our mate Google, 72 per cent of couples who find their way back to one another end up being together for good, so hey, I hope this is it. I would live forever if living was with her. Turns out she was my person all along. J, you are the meaning of love to me – always have been, always will be.

Obviously, I was worried about work when I came back to Manchester, as London is apparently 'the place to be'. I can confirm, that is not true. Work has been poppin' off since I got home. I'm filming, writing, recording and truly living out the start of my dreams, and I know it's only up from here.

I'm starting to acknowledge that I now might be an . . . *adult*? I've never felt like one before. I'm twenty-five, but still feel sixteen in my head. The only real difference is I've gained a bit of weight and I understand how a credit card works. If you're reading this wondering when the fuck you'll get your life together, *don't*. I've discovered it doesn't work like that. I think even proper adults feel like we do. We're all just trying to get by and be as happy as we can be. Don't forget that we just exist on a rock that floats in space; that always makes me feel better.

Just remember:

1. Dreams require sacrifice (wanky thing to say, but very true nevertheless).
2. Stop giving a fuck what others think about you. It's not their life, it's yours.
3. Embrace failure. You can cry about it, but know when to pattern the fuck up and try again.
4. Do not give up. Life is fucking shit and hard, and if you give up, somebody else will get there first. Don't let them.
5. Do whatever makes you happy; doesn't matter what it is (unless it's murder, maybe don't do that).

6. Love yourself. You have to be your number-one fan and advocate.
7. You're not always supposed to get everything you want. I've missed out on opportunities before, and later on realised something better was round the corner.
8. Nobody else knows what the fuck they're doing.
9. Wank often; it makes you feel better, even if it's just for a fleeting moment.
10. Invest in experiences, not things. Go on holiday; memories last forever (unless you get dementia).

I feel like we've been on quite a journey together. I wanted to write this book for Luke. I set myself a little challenge that I could do it for him; he continues to be the reason for everything that I do, and I'd like to believe that a part of him lives on in me, so as long as I'm here making history, so is he. He would find it hard to believe that I had written a book, unless he knew that the book was essentially all about me. That's easier to process, I think. Unless you're my family, I guess you didn't know him, the same way you might not know me – but I hope now you do. I hope that at least something among these pages will stick with you – even if it's me shitting in the snow and stabbing my helpless fish to death.

Thanks for sticking with me until the end. Kinda weird, innit? What will you do now? Are you going to pass this book on to a mate? Let it collect dust on a shelf? Take it to the charity shop? Use the blank pages to write your shopping lists? Reread it? I imagine by this point in the book (drink!) you're absolutely hammered, so I'm going to be totally honest here, I don't know how to end this. I just googled 'how to finish a book', and apparently, you're supposed to write the ending at the start?

Nobody fucking told me!

Acknowledgements

It feels really cool to write acknowledgements. I know I'll read this and be annoyed that I've forgotten so many people, so basically thank you to everyone. ☺

In no particular order, I would like to thank my amazing editor Briony Gowlett for believing in me and this silly little book; you've been a dream – and all of the team at Radar for helping make this possible. The world's best agent Dawn Sedgwick, for consistently championing me and everything I do, despite me messaging her all hours of the night on WhatsApp. Molly Seymour, for being not only a talented producer, but a lovely friend. Thank you for inviting me for my first general and helping me get my foot in a very heavy door.

Thank you to my family. I'm sorry we've had such a shit time, but I'm also thankful for the best times. I wouldn't swap any of you for the world (not even you, Matthew). Thank you, Stacey, for being my rock when I've needed it the most. I love you all more than you'll ever know. Also, sorry to my dad. There's a lot in this book you didn't know, but hey ho, better late than never! To Luke, for being my best mate and my biggest inspiration. I love you and I miss you for the rest of time.

Thank you to my friends, who have put up with so many different versions of me. Gemma, I don't know how I would have gotten through life without you, thank you for being there whenever I've needed you. You are one in a million. Danny and Sam – my favourite men, I'm so lucky to have you both. Danny for never failing to make me laugh and Sam for being the kindest soul. My exes, I'm sorry I broke your hearts. Neither of you deserved that. (Hoping you'll find that funny.) Seriously though, thank you for the memories.

Last but by no means least, July. Thank you for keeping the book juicy! Kidding, thank you for being the one. I love you endlessly x